The Campus Site

The Campus Site

A Prehistoric Camp at Fairbanks, Alaska

by
Charles M. Mobley

University of Alaska Press

Library of Congress Cataloging-in-Publication Data

Mobley, Charles M.
    The Campus Site : a prehistoric camp at Fairbanks, Alaska / by
Charles M. Mobley.
      p. cm.
    Includes bibliographical references.
    ISBN 0-912006-48-X (alk. paper)
    1. Campus Site (Fairbanks, Alaska)   2. Paleo-Indians—Alaska—Fairbanks.   3. Fairbanks (Alaska)—Antiqui-
ties. I. Title
E78.A3M67   1991
979.8′6—dc20

                                                                 90-29894
                                                                    CIP

International Standard Book Number: cloth 912006-48-X
                                               paper 912006-52-8
Library of Congress Catalogue Number: 90-29894

Printed in the United States.
Typeset in the United States by Graphic Composition, Inc.

This publication was printed on acid-free paper which meets the minimum requirements of American National Standard
for Information Sciences-Permanence of Paper for Printed Library Materials, ANSI Z39.48 –1984.

Publication coordination by Debbie Van Stone.
Publication design by Robert C. Emmett of Northern Publication Services.
Cover design by Dixon Jones, IMPACT Graphics, UAF Rasmuson Library.

ABSTRACT

The Campus Site is an archaeological site on the grounds of the University of Alaska at Fairbanks, Alaska. Stone artifacts found there since 1933 include microblades and microblade cores similar to those found in Siberia, northern China, and Japan. The site was announced as the first evidence in support of the Bering Land Bridge hypothesis for human entrance into North America from Asia, and later was assigned to the 12,000–8,000 year old Denali Complex. A restudy of the specimens indicates the site to have a wider variety of artifacts, reflecting microblade, macroblade, biface, and core/flake technologies. These artifacts were sometimes retouched, or made into burins. Reported here are the first radiocarbon dates from the Campus Site, indicating use about 3,000 years ago. Many artifact illustrations and historic photographs are used with an analysis of the specimens and notes, to produce a basic descriptive report on the Campus Site.

Le Site "Campus" est un site archéologique sur les terrains de l'Université d'Alaska à Fairbanks, Alaska. Les artefacts de pierre que l'on y découvre depuis 1933 comprennent des noyaux de microlames et des microlames semblables à ceux que l'on a découverts en Sibérie, en Chine septentrionale et au Japon. Le Site fut annoncé comme la première évidence à l'appui de l'hypothèse du Pont Terrestre Bering pour l'entrée en Amérique du nord de l'homme venant d'Asie. Le site fut associé depuis au Complexe Denali qui date de 12,000 à 8,000 ans. Une nouvelle étude des spécimens indique que le Site possède une plus ample variété d'artefacts qui révèlent les technologies microlame, macrolame, biface et noyau/flocon. Ces artefacts étaient quelquefois retouchés ou tournés en burins. Dans cette étude se trouvent les premières dates de radiocarbone du Site "Campus" qui indiquent l'usage il y a environ 3,000 ans. De nombreuses illustrations des artefacts et des photographies historiques sont présentées avec une analyse des spécimens et des notes pour rendre une description de base du Site "Campus."

Стоянка Кампуса располагается на территории занятой сейчас Университетом Аляски в г. Фербенксе. Камменые орудия обнаруженные здесь начиная с 1933 г. включают микропластинки и микронуклеусы сходные на те что найденные в Северной Азии. Считалось, что эта стоянка была первым достоверным подтверждением гипотезы заселения Америки из Азии по Берингоморской суши. Позднее она была отнесена к комплексу Денали, датированному 8,000-12,000 л.н. Повторное обследование находок показало что на стоянке представлен гораздо более широкий спектр артифактов, отражающий технологии микропластинков, пластинков, бифасов и нуклеусов отщепов. Эти артифакты были иногда ретушированные, или сделанные в резцы. В отчете приводится первая радиоуглеродная датировка университетской площадки занятой лет 3,000 назад. Отчет представляет собой полное и весьма детальное описание университетской площадки; он снабжен многочисленными рисунками артифактов, снимками и анализом отдельных находок.

El sitio 'Campus' es un sitio arqueológico localizado en el recinto de la Universidad de Alaska en Fairbanks, Alaska. Los artefactos de piedra que se han encontrado allí desde 1933 incluyen núcleos de microhojas y microhojas, parecidos a los que se han encontrado en Siberia, el norte de China y Japón. El sitio se anunció como la primera evidencia en apoyo a la hipótesis del puente de tierra Beringio, propuesta para explicar la entreada en América del Norte del hombre venido de Asia; posteriormente se lo determinó como parte del Complejo Denali, de 12,000 a 8,000 años. Un estudio nuevo de los especímenes indica que el sitio tiene una variedad amplia de artefactos, reflejando las tecnologías microhoja, macrohoja, biface, y núcleo-lasca. De vez en cuando los artefactos se encontraron retocados o convertidos en buriles. En el estudio se presentan los primeros datos de radiocarbono del sitio 'Campus,' indicando su empleo hace aproximadamente 3,000 años. Se usan muchas ilustraciones de los artefactos y fotografías históricas, con apuntes y un análisis de los especímenes, para producir un trabajo descriptivo básico sobre el sitio 'Campus.'

キャンパスサイトはアラスカ大学フェアバンクス校にある古跡である。 1933年から発見されている石器には、シベリア、中国北部及び日本で発見されたものと似たマイクロブレイド（小石刀）やマイクロブレイド・コア（小石刀の芯）が含まれている。 この敷地はアジアから北米へ人口が流入したというベーリング・ランドブリッジ説を裏付ける最初の証拠として発表され、後に 12,000--8,000年デナリ・コンプレックスに割りあてられた。標本の再調査は、この敷地にはマイクロブレイド（小石刀）、マクロブレイド（大石刀）、バイフェイス（二面刀）、コア・フレイク（芯・破片）の技術を反映する多種多様な人工物があることを示している。 これらの人工物は時々加工されたり、発火具に改良されたりした。 ここでは、約 3000年前の使用を示すキャンパスサイトからの最初の放射性炭素年代が報告されている。 多くの人工物の絵図や歴史的重要な写真は標本、記録の分析とともにキャンパスサイトの基本的記述的報告を作り出すために使われている。

TABLE OF CONTENTS

LIST OF ILLUSTRATIONS

LIST OF TABLES

PREFACE

Today, Alaska consists of a diverse mix of ethnic groups, including indigenous Natives who have lived there for thousands of years. When Russian explorers began trade and settlement in the late 1700s, approximately 80,000 Natives inhabited the area between the Arctic Ocean and the islands of southeast Alaska, and between the Aleutian Islands and that region now known as the Yukon Territory of Canada. The Russians, other Europeans and the Americans that sailed Alaska's waters during the subsequent decades noted the similarities in language and lifestyles that linked the Inupiat Eskimo of northern Alaska to related people around the pole in Canada, Greenland, and Russia. They were observed to be different, linguistically and culturally, from the Aleuts that the Russians first encountered in the Aleutian Islands and Alaska Peninsula. In between, extending from the Bering Sea to Prince William Sound, were people with varying adaptations to the environment, but speaking variants of one language, Yupik. In central Alaska, distant from most coastlines, lived small bands of Athabascans speaking a language strongly related to that of interior Native American groups through western Canada and even to the Apache and Navajo of the American Southwest. And in southeast Alaska lived the Tlingit and Haida, who—although having distinctive languages—shared many cultural patterns, such as large dugout canoes and a rich carving tradition, with other coastal Native groups living in the areas now known as British Columbia and the states of Washington and Oregon.

But the antiquity of some of these Native groups was unknown. The Haida in far southeast Alaska were considered in the oral history of the region to have moved into Alaska from the Queen Charlotte Islands of British Columbia, not too many generations earlier. The very close similarity of the Inupiat language to that of other Inuit groups in the circumpolar Arctic also suggested recent migrations of these wide-spread peoples from a common stock. But the Yupik, the Athabascans, and the Aleut all seemed to have occupied their lands for eons, developing a long tradition of hunting and gathering patterns that served them well. These peoples had well-crafted, time-tested stories of their origins, handed down from generation to generation as oral history. Yet for the philosophers and scientists of the early industrial world the antiquity of Alaska Natives, like that of all the indigenous peoples of North, Middle, and South America, was largely a matter of conjecture until the application of the radiocarbon dating technique developed in the 1940s.

That conjecture began soon after Europeans arrived in the New World. At that time Europe was experiencing the revival of classical values in art and literature, and ancient lands were valued as a source of monumental sculpture and art. Artifacts from Greece, Italy, Egypt, and other far-off places were acquired by adventurers and explorers, sometimes from burial chambers and tombs, to be admired by their patrons when the objects arrived in Europe. As scientific inquiry became an accepted avocation of the rich, explorations were conducted to acquire information as well. Earth-covered boulder tombs called barrows, scattered across the estates of northern Europe, were often the subject of weekend excursions in which hired hands dug up bones and artifacts for admiration and study by their aristocratic supervisors.

North America seemed to have some barrows of its own. Comparing the large earth mounds of New England and the Ohio River Valley with the less spectacular architecture of the indigenous living peoples they met, visitors to the New World posed a question. Were the native inhabitants of North America the descendants of the anonymous mound-builders? In one of the first controlled archaeological excavations in the New World, Thomas Jefferson dug into a mound on his estate at Monticello to satisfy his curiosity about that question, coming to the conclusion that there was a link between the past and present indigenous cultures. That posed a second question: How did the original Natives come to occupy the New World?

The answer to that question lay in the realm of prehistory, the time before written records were kept. It was known from Egyptian hieroglyphic texts that the world was several thousand years old, and a Cambridge scholar had calculated the exact year of origin as 4004 B.C. But in the late 1800s, as Charles Darwin's ideas of biological evolution became generally accepted by learned individuals, fossil evidence was viewed as supporting a much greater antiquity for the planet and the life it supported. Specimens from Asia and Africa suggested that much of human evolution took place there. So it was likely that the presence of humans in the New World was the result of migrations from the Old. Who was responsible? There was no shortage of candidates. Egyptians, Phoenicians, Polynesians, the lost tribes of Israel, and survivors of the lost continent of Atlantis were included as potential sources for the colonization. An alternative view was that the Native Americans had come from Asia, crossing the Bering Strait where that continent comes close to the northwest tip of North America.

In the early decades of the 20th century, the new multifaceted discipline of anthropology began its debut at selected universities in the United States. Archaeologists, developing painstaking techniques for recovering information from buried prehistoric sites and new methods of interpretation, began to lay the foundation for a scientific understanding of human prehistory. One of the first widely publicized excavations using the stratigraphic method, which recognized the layers of soil in a cultural site as a source of information on changing cultural patterns through time, was by Nels Nelson at a pueblo site in the American Southwest. By the 1930s, prehistoric cultures termed Clovis and Folsom were identified in the archaeo-

logical record in association with bones of now-extinct animals such as mammoth. Based on this and geological evidence it was supposed that people had inhabited the New World for perhaps as long as 10,000 years.

In Alaska, archaeology had to share the spotlight with ethnology, since there were living cultures with exotic traditions that were considered to be as interesting as prehistoric peoples. Some of the first systematic archaeological efforts were conducted by Otto Geist on St. Lawrence Island, and by Frederica de Laguna in Prince William Sound, in the 1930s. The center of higher education in the territory of Alaska was the Agricultural College and School of Mines, in Fairbanks. And there occurred events—in prehistory and history—that form the subject of this book. At the Campus Site, over 50 years ago, the first evidence in firm support for the Bering land bridge hypothesis for human origins in the New World was found.

ACKNOWLEDGMENTS

Many people have generously given me assistance and encouragement in the years since the autumn of 1981, when I asked a colleague at the University of Alaska Fairbanks if he could suggest a moth-balled archaeological collection worthy of descriptive analysis. Almost everyone I know in the Alaska archaeological community has helped in some way, by giving me space to live or work in, by suggesting references to consult, by offering insights into the data or providing new data, by helping me find the funds for radiocarbon dating and other analysis, by critiquing my illustrations and manuscript drafts, or by simply looking forward to the results. The excavators of the 1930s and 1960s enthusiastically gave me their original notes and personal accounts. My friends and family have un-selfishly granted me the time necessary to see the Campus Site restudy to completion. I thank you all very, very much. Over the decades the Campus Site has become communal property—a source of information for numerous researchers; it is fitting that so many individuals have had a part in the making of this book. Direct funding or services for parts of this research were provided by (the former) Alaska Division of Geological and Geophysical Surveys, Alaska Heritage Research Group, (the former) Alaska Historical Commission, Albert Dickey, Sheldon Jackson College and the University of Alaska Museum Geist Fund. Finally, with much affection, I dedicate this book to my son, Ottar.

INTRODUCTION

In his New York office one November day in 1934, several years after the return of the American Museum of Natural History's acclaimed Central Asiatic Expedition, Staff Anthropologist Nels Nelson opened a small heavy box postmarked Fairbanks, Alaska. Inside were a number of tiny stone artifacts excavated from a shallow site on the grounds of the Alaska Agricultural College and School of Mines, at Fairbanks. Nelson's subsequent proclamation startled the scientific world, for ". . . about twenty small semi-conical flint cores and several end-scrapers . . . are identical in several respects with thousands of specimens found in the Gobi desert . . . [and] furnish the first clear archaeological evidence we have of early migration to the American continent . . ." (Nelson 1935:356). The Bering land bridge hypothesis for human colonization of the New World was now supported by fact.

The Campus Site, as it came to be called, was excavated sporadically through the 1930s, in 1966–1967, and again in 1971. Preliminary articles by Nelson (1935, 1937) and Froelich Rainey (1939, 1940) were consulted in North America, the Soviet Union, and Japan (Mochanov 1969:101, Dikov 1965:13, Befu and Chard 1960:842). The archaeological collections were dispersed to Moscow, New York, Ottawa, Tucson, and Fairbanks. The Campus Site is the type site for a microblade technique of stone working in the New World, producing the small microblade cores known as "Campus-type" cores. West (1967:361) declared that "the Campus Site represents the most important single landmark in the history of interior Alaskan archaeology." Yet despite its fame, involving numerous excavations and dozens of secondary references in the archaeological literature, a complete synthesis of the Campus Site has never been written. This problem has long been recognized; for example, Mauger (1970:11) laments that "no complete report has been issued on the material and so the collection has the dubious distinction of being frequently mentioned but having little of a substantive nature written about it." The bluff on which the site is located was eventually surmounted by a large totem pole and bounded by buildings, parking lots, streets, and sidewalks of the University of Alaska Fairbanks.

Location and Natural Environment

The University of Alaska campus is on the west side of Fairbanks, in central Alaska (Figure 1). Formerly, the area was a separate community known as College, but urban growth has merged it into the city of Fairbanks. The university has grown to encompass a hill of several hundred acres, overlooking the broad Tanana River floodplain to the south. The site is located on the brow of that hill, at the extreme southeast margin of the campus.

Fairbanks is at the contact between two physiographic provinces—the Yukon-Tanana Uplands to the north, and the Tanana-Kuskokwim Lowlands to the south (Wahrhaftig 1965:24, 29). The Tanana River, one of interior Alaska's major rivers, has a watershed extending from the Canadian border northwest to its confluence with the Yukon River, a distance of over 600 km (Figure 1). The Chena River, draining a portion of the Yukon-Tanana Uplands to the east, joins the Tanana River just a few km downstream from Fairbanks. A now-inactive slough of the Chena River lies just below the Campus Site at the base of the bluff.

The Quaternary geology shows that the Fairbanks area was not glaciated, but it did accumulate considerable glacially-derived sediment from the glacial rivers draining the northern flanks of the Alaska Range (Péwé 1965a:37–38). Undifferentiated loess (wind-borne glacial silt), silt, sand, and gravel of Pleistocene age comprise the Tanana Lowlands, while the Yukon-Tanana Uplands contains exposures of silt, loess, and Birch Creek schist (Péwé et al. 1975). Hilltops and south-facing slopes are the only locations in which permafrost is not present (Péwé 1965b:10). A mantle of massive, unbedded Fairbanks Loess, up to 80 feet thick, is present on the university grounds, although it is less than one meter thick at the Campus Site itself. The loess is of Wisconsin and Illinoian age, and contains several thin layers of volcanic ash (Péwé 1965b:14–15).

The silt loam, decomposed from micaceous loess, forms part of a broad sheet of similar soils in central Alaska termed "Subarctic Brown Forest Soils" (DeMent 1962:6). Generalizing about the University of Alaska campus, Péwé (1965b:15) describes the soil in part as follows:

> Loess on hilltops and upper and middle slopes gives rise to a brown soil termed the Subarctic Brown Forest soil. . . . The upper horizons are not dark and mixed with organic debris because organisms necessary for mixing are absent and because of the slow rate of decay of organic matter. . . . The Subarctic Brown Forest soils are youthful and relatively stable in their environment.

The soil at the specific Campus Site locale is classified as Gilmore silt loam, according to the official soil survey for the Fairbanks area (Rieger et al. 1963:Map Sheet #10).

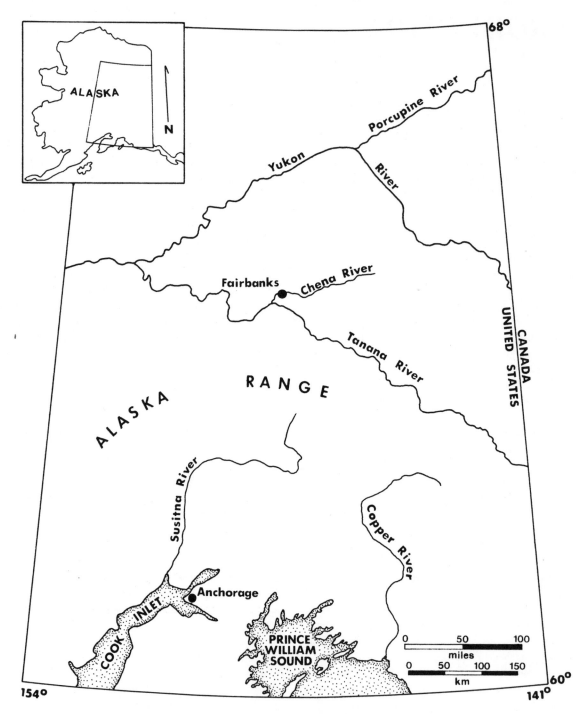

Figure 1. Map of central Alaska, showing major rivers and location of Fairbanks.

The present vegetation of the Fairbanks area is dominated by quaking aspen, paper birch, black spruce, and white spruce trees, with larch and balsam poplar in the lowland areas (Little and Viereck 1974). Alder and willow thickets intermingle with the stands of trees, and shrubs include highbush cranberry, Labrador tea, prickly rose, and dwarf blueberry. Although the Campus Site has experienced considerable development around and partially over it, most of these species can still be found there.

Game animals present in the Fairbanks area (some now in reduced numbers since EuroAmerican settlement) include moose, black and brown bear, arctic hare, spruce grouse, squirrels, and fur bearers such as mink, muskrat, beaver, marten, otter, lynx, fox, wolverine, and wolf (Alaska Department of Fish and Game 1973, 1978a). Migratory waterfowl are seasonally available. Seasonal runs of king salmon and chum salmon are found in both the Chena and Tanana Rivers, and the latter also contains coho salmon (Alaska Department of Fish and Game 1978b). Perennially available in both watercourses are sheefish, northern pike, burbot, grayling, and whitefish (Alaska Department of Fish and Game 1978c).

The climate of the Fairbanks area, like much of Alaska's interior, is cold and dry. Temperatures range from −66 degrees F in the winter to 99 degrees F in the summer (Hartman n.d.). Average precipitation is 12 inches per year, two-thirds of which falls between May and September (Johnson et al. 1979:9). The latitude of Fairbanks, 200 km south of the Arctic Circle, provides for almost 22 daylight hours at the summer solstice, and corresponding darkness in the winter (Rieger et al. 1963:2).

The Holocene paleoenvironment of the Fairbanks area is pertinent to interpretation of the Campus Site, since the archaeological deposits have been estimated to date as old as 8,000 to 12,000 B.P. (West 1975). Central Alaska experienced a warming trend at about 10,000 B.P., as part of a global climatic shift, at which time forests developed in the Fairbanks area (Péwé 1975a). The peak of this trend was a thermal maximum sometime between 7,500–3,500 B.P., during which the snowline rose, the permafrost table fell, and vegetation patterns shifted slightly (Péwé 1975b:113), Central Alaska cooled somewhat after the thermal maximum, resulting in glacial advance up to about 300–200 B.P., followed by a warming period up to the present (Péwé 1975b:121). In central Alaska "the vegetation type present today was essentially established within 1,000 or 2,000 years after the Holocene began" (Péwé 1975b:122). "In the Fairbanks area no bones of extinct vertebrates have been found in post-Wisconsin sediments. . . . only bones of living forms have been found," including "rare finds of *Bison bison*" (Péwé 1975b:101).

In summary, for the last 10,000 years the environment of the Fairbanks area has included more or less the same general suite of plant and animal species that is present in modern times, although there is evidence for minor climatic fluctuation during that time.

Goals of the Campus Site Restudy Project

Designing the Campus Site restudy project required careful decisions about what questions to exclude from consideration, as well as attention to questions that could be evaluated using the existing collections. Without firsthand excavation experience at the site, the author relied on the observations of others in regard to site stratigraphy, excavation method, and other field matters. Through the years the standards for field notes and other supporting documentation were set by several investigators with differing theoretical and methodological backgrounds, and the resulting quality and quantity of information varies from excavation to excavation. Catalog discrepancies were

inevitable given the different standards and institutions involved, and the many years of handling that some artifacts received. All these factors restricted the ways in which the current analyses could be conducted.

Certain questions about the Campus Site have puzzled researchers for many years. The apparent lack of natural or cultural stratigraphy and the variety of tool forms recovered raised the issue of contemporaneity. Does the Campus Site represent one major occupation or several? On typological grounds (mainly the microblade assemblage) the site was thought to date to between 12,000 and 8,000 B.P. (West 1967, 1975), but no chronometric dating had been attempted beyond an undocumented obsidian hydration assay (Bandi 1969:52; West 1981:142). These two questions—the contemporaneity and absolute dating of the Campus Site material—are of much interest to scholars, and yet are also the most difficult to resolve. While information pertaining to both issues has resulted from the Campus Site restudy, their resolution was not the primary goal.

Thorough description of the artifact assemblage was considered to be the most realistically attainable result of the restudy. Despite the sequence of excavations undertaken at the site, the only primary literature available consists of short published reports from the 1930s work (Nelson 1935, 1937; Rainey 1939, 1940), and unpublished manuscripts resulting from the excavations of 1966 and 1967 (Hosley 1968; Hosley and Mauger 1967; Mauger 1970, 1971). Some good comparative treatments of Alaskan archaeological assemblages use information from Campus Site specimens (Irving 1955; Cook 1968; Sanger 1968a; Morlan 1970), but in all cases only particular artifact types were analyzed, and usually only the material retained by the University of Alaska Museum was consulted. A comprehensive description of all the artifacts residing in each accessible curating institution was judged useful, since the Campus Site is a type site of the Denali Complex (West 1967), and has been referred to in a comparative context by many researchers.

To compliment the prosaic description, illustration was a focus of the restudy project. With its traditional emphasis on culture-historical reconstruction, understanding Alaskan archaeology and its literature has required personal familiarity with the various type assemblages of artifacts. At the University of Alaska Museum, the Campus Site assemblage has always been one of the most-requested collections for viewing by visiting scholars, contributing to the worn appearance of selected artifacts (and perhaps, over the years, some curators). Many researchers have published Campus Site artifacts in photographs or pen-and-ink illustrations (Nelson 1937, Rainey 1939, Irving 1955, Hayashi 1968, Smith 1974, Del Bene 1980, Bandi 1969, West 1967, 1981, Aigner 1986), but usually the same ones are published time and again (no more than thirty have been figured), and in no case has the range of variability been depicted in any one source. As a consequence, published illustrations have served to downplay the assemblage variability. For example, Specimen 03–16 (Figure 17, c), which is one of the most delicately flaked microblade cores in the collection, has been figured at least seven times, called "a representative core" (Del Bene 1980:34), and said "to depict the range of blade cores present in particular assemblages" (West 1981:90). One single plate of line drawings depicting the same three microblade cores, three retouched specimens, five microblades, and a biface, has been published three separate times (Bandi 1969:51, West 1981:140, Aigner 1986:134). Consequently, an illustrated catalog of the lithic tools and technology was judged useful as part of the restudy, much in the manner of a final site report.

Thus the primary goal was to compile available information and make it available in a site report format, emphasizing the artifact assemblages through description and illustration. Additional information was acquired and applied to the issues of contemporaneity and absolute dating of the Campus Site, but—as is common with restudy projects (Sampson 1978)—it did not completely resolve

those issues. Critics and scholars of Arctic and subarctic prehistory will, however, have available more information with which to support their claims.

Organization of the Volume

The organization of this volume reflects the various emphases of the restudy. The following chapter presents a history of fieldwork, highlighting the important information contributed by each phase of excavation. The distribution of the records and artifact collections is then traced, with comments about their current state of curation. Mention is made of the methods used to achieve the goals of the restudy project, including a presentation of terms and definitions used in the lithic artifact analysis. A qualitative and quantitative analysis of the Campus Site artifacts forms the body of the volume. The issues of contemporaneity and dating the Campus Site, and the activities taking place there in prehistoric times, are taken up in turn. Finally, the various lines of evidence are used to reconsider the character of the Campus Site as compared to the way others have depicted it in previous studies.

HISTORY OF FIELDWORK

Discovery (1933–1935)

Archaeological study in Alaska did not begin in earnest until the late 1920s—relatively recently compared to some other parts of North America. Early explorers and ethnographers had recorded occasional abandoned historic/prehistoric villages, but the older record of man's activity was unknown. Indeed, this was the case for the entire New World, for it was not until the discovery of the PaleoIndian Clovis and Folsom complexes in the American Southwest, during the late 1920s, that the antiquity of man in the Americas was strongly supported (Howard 1935, Hrdlička 1936). Even then, the radiocarbon method was not available to provide an absolute date for such sites. Were they 4,000 years old? Or 40,000 years old? Furthermore, where did the American natives come from? The similarity of American arctic peoples to those of Siberia indicated that migrations had occurred from northern Asia across the Bering Strait, but the antiquity of such migrations was unknown. Man's date of arrival in the New World and his origin were two major issues being considered by North American archaeologists of the time.

Published accounts state that stone artifacts bearing on both of these questions were discovered in the fall of 1933 in a post hole dug on the campus of the Alaska Agricultural College and School of Mines (now the University of Alaska) in Fairbanks. The discoverer—a student named James C. Jacobsen—reported the find to university president Dr. Charles E. Bunnell. The site was not formally investigated until the following year. A letter to the author from alumnus Wilson W. Walton, however, states that "flint chippings" had been found there as early as 1931 or 1932.

The first controlled excavations at the Campus Site were conducted by two Fairbanks students—John (Jack) Dorsh and Albert Dickey. Both were employed by Childs Frick of the American Museum of Natural History to collect Pleistocene fauna specimens washed out by the several placer gold operations of the Fairbanks Exploration Company—a task that Dorsh continued for Frick after World War II (Keim 1969:256). In July of 1934 a water shortage on the creeks forced the mining company to reduce their hydraulic activity, thus lessening the number of paleontological specimens uncovered. Dr. Bunnell suggested that the men explore the area on the campus where artifacts had been found the year before. In a letter to the author, Mr. Dickey writes:

> We made several test cuts and finally located a surprising concentration of worked stone material. At first we used small tools and brushes to remove the artifacts. But soon we were convinced that the stuff was simply scattered, not stratified. . . . Then we set up a large screen and went in for mass production. Whenever the bone business was slow, Jack and I would work the dig. . . . At the end of the first season, a gallon can of artifacts was sent to Dr. Nelson.

John Dorsh evidently prepared a report on the 1934 excavations, a portion of which was printed in the September (1934) edition of the campus newspaper—the *Farthest North Collegian* (12:(12):1,8):

> Last fall a rude arrowhead was turned from the bottom of a post hole on a low bluff overlooking the floor of the Tanana Valley, about 100 yards to the southeast of the Administration Building. On July 7 we started an excavation on the extreme brow of the bluff and worked a cut up through the overburden to a point about ten feet above the site of discovery, a distance of roughly 40 feet, removing all topsoil to the bedrock. We recovered about two dozen worked pieces of flint, obsidian, quartz, and chalcedony, and two hammer stones. One hammer stone was found in place, the other was picked up adjacent to the excavation. Several hundred chips and flakes of the same kind of rock were also found. Some of the pieces were very well shaped projectile points. About 1,500 square feet of bedrock was exposed making an estimated total of 70 cubic yards of material removed.
>
> The artifacts and chips average about eight inches below the surface, and the average of the soil mantle is about 15 inches. The depth of the tool making rocks increases toward the brow of the hill. In some places the depth approaches 14 inches for the worked rocks. Only one possible fireplace was discovered, but due to the fact that the stones were found under the ashes of a modern bonfire nothing can be said definitely regarding this. Some few fragments of bone have also been found and a fragment of a tooth.

The Dr. Nelson referred to in Dickey's account was Nels C. Nelson, an archaeologist at the American Museum of Natural History. Although the container sent to him held only approximately 400 artifacts, he noticed similarities between them and artifacts collected in the Gobi Desert of Mongolia (Nelson 1926:247–251, 1935:356):

> On examination . . . the collection proved to contain, besides hammerstones, chipped projectile points, and numerous reject flakes, about twenty

Figure 2. Excavators of the Campus Site in 1935, with paleontological material collected from placer deposits in the Goldstream area, near Fairbanks. Pictured are Archibald B. Roosevelt, Jr., Albert H. Dickey, John Dorsh, and Walter Sullivan. The photograph was taken by J. Louis Giddings using Dorsh's camera.

small semi-conical flint cores, and several small endscrapers. These last mentioned items, the cores and the small endscrapers, are of special interest because they are identical in several respects with thousands of specimens found in the Gobi desert by the Central Asiatic Expedition in 1925–28. The specimens furnish the first clear archaeological evidence we have of early migration to the American continent, apparently during the final or Azilian-Tardenoisian stage of the Paleolithic culture horizon, possibly 7,000–10,000 B.C.

Nelson's remarks were widely noted and reprinted in the popular press, including the *Farthest North Collegian*, and he elaborated upon his view after examining new material acquired through excavations at the Campus Site in 1935.

The 1935 excavations were again conducted by Jack Dorsh and Albert Dickey, executed sporadically between paleontological collecting expeditions financed by the American Museum of Natural History. Two young assistants were sent from New York to help in the summer's work (Figure 2). Archibald B. Roosevelt, Jr.—a grandson of Theodore Roosevelt—was sent to Alaska under the sponsorship of Childs Frick by virtue of a long friendship between Frick and Archibald B. Roosevelt, Sr. While he found it an exciting and rewarding experience, involvement with the project did not particularly affect Roosevelt's career—he later became an intelligence officer for the government, and Vice-President of International Relations for the Chase Manhattan Bank (Roosevelt 1988). According to his account (Roosevelt, personal communication), the excavation trenches at the Campus Site also doubled as traps for mice and shrews, which fell in and were promptly caught and stuffed for the collections of the American Museum of Natural History. A schoolmate of Roosevelt's was also sent to Alaska to work on the project.

In a letter to the author, Walter Sullivan writes: "We were inexperienced teenagers, but the trip probably determined the final course of my career in a variety of ways." He later became senior science editor of the *New York Times*.

With a total of four men, crew leader John Dorsh was able to alternate two-man teams between the Campus Site excavations and the fauna recovery work at the placer operations, according to personal diaries in the possession of his wife—Mrs. Bertha Dorsh. This greatly increased the number of artifacts available for study to over 800 specimens (Table 1), and the list of raw materials recognized was expanded to include "quartz, quartzite, basanite, chert, jasper, obsidian, and moss agate." The new sample was sent to Nels Nelson, who prepared for the journal *American Antiquity* a more comprehensive paper that included two line drawings illustrating three endscrapers, three cores, and three microblades (Nelson 1937).

Excavations in 1936

In September of 1936 Dr. Froelich G. Rainey began further excavations at the site as part of the new college course entitled "Arctic Archaeology." His account of the site, published as part of the article "Archaeology in Central Alaska" in the *Anthropological Papers of the American Museum of Natural History*, has remained the primary reference to the site for over 50 years (Rainey 1939: 381–383):

> . . . trenches have been run along the brow of the hill for a distance of some thirty meters and at right angles, toward the west, for a distance of twenty meters. Flint flakes and tools have been found in all sections removed. Test pits have been dug in the adjacent field at various points within a radius of one hundred meters; in most cases, these have produced at least scattered flint chippings. Furthermore, fragments of stone implements and flint flakes have been picked up on the surface over a large part of College Hill which has been under cultivation from time to time. . . . There is, however, a marked concentration of material in a limited area near the point where the first implement was found. This section extends along the brink of the steep incline which descends from the hilltop to the floor of the Tanana Valley, twenty meters below.
>
> The series of trenches dug during the past three seasons represent the removal of approximately one hundred twenty cubic meters of deposit. All trenches have been excavated to the depth of bedrock which at this point, however, never lies more than forty centimeters below the surface. A thin layer of turf or humus, not more than ten centimeters in depth, covers a shallow stratum of fine, reddish, residual material which, in turn, rests on the

Table 1. Artifact inventory of 1934 and 1935 Campus Site collections, from Nelson (1937:267–272).

3 bones
1 hammerstone
1 oblong rubbing stone of red tufa
500 angular flakes, small to medium
63 used flakes
77 flakes with chipped margins
2 oblong pointed flakes wsith marginal chipping
1 chopping tool or scraper
21 side scrapers
19 small to medium sized end scrapers
3 biface blanks suitable for knives or spear points
22 knives or spear points
3 arrow points (1 each: straight base, simple stemmed, side notched)
31 small semi-conical or polyhedral cores for small prismatic blades
29 small prismatic blades

> decomposed bedrock of schist. None of the deposit which I have removed contained habitation refuse other than stone implements. There is no bone refuse and no soil blackened with organic decay. Bits of charcoal are scattered through the soil, but there are no hearths or other ash deposits. At one time the University held the annual student bonfire on the crest of this hill. . . . and from time to time refuse has been burned here. This accounts for the ash on the surface and may be responsible for the bone fragments in the collections. . . .
>
> . . . we removed the deposit in ten centimeter layers and found implements, fragments, and chips both in the surface turf and in the subsoil. The majority of objects, however, lay in the subsoil at depths of from ten to thirty centimeters. Each trench dug was divided into sections measuring three by three meters. As many as forty objects, including chips, fragments, and complete tools were found in some of these sections, while others contained no more than a half dozen. In no case, however, was there a cache or pocket of chips and tools.
>
> The depth at which the specimens were found has no bearing on their age, since it is possible that surface soil has been eroding rather than accumulating on this abrupt hillside. Furthermore, the formation of soil in this region is an exceedingly slow process. The absence of house site depressions and of bone or ash deposits does not necessarily indicate great age, since the site may have been simply a workshop rather than a habitation.

The 1936 excavations provided a sample of approximately 500 artifacts, including 81 classified as tools (Table 2). Raw materials recognized were "flint, obsidian, fine-grained basalt, quartz, quartzite, and jasper." Rainey described the tools within each category, often individually, and illustrated thirty artifacts in two photographic

Table 2. Artifact inventory of the 1936 Campus Site collections, from Rainey (1939:383).

29 retouched flakes
 4 complete blades
 6 fragmentary blades
 2 side scrapers
 4 end scrapers
 2 cleavers
 3 microblade cores
31 microblades

plates. The small size and lack of cortex on the cores was noted (three were illustrated), and their three major characteristics were pointed out: "lateral flutings formed by the removal of small prismatic flakes, a striking platform, and transverse preparatory flaking" (Rainey 1939:387). Measurements of microblades were given as 1.5–4.0 cm in length, and 1–2 mm in width (although he may have meant one-two mm in thickness). Rainey commented that some microblades were probably missed due to the coarseness of the ¼ inch mesh screen (Rainey 1939:388).

Rainey compared the Campus Site microblade industry with that found at the upper Tanana River site of Dixthada (see Shinkwin 1979), in which he had also conducted excavations, noting that the protohistoric affinity of the latter implied a late date for the Campus Site (at least relative

to the microblade tradition in Asia). Small end scrapers were common in both Alaskan assemblages, but "the semi-lunar side scrapers retouched on one face only, the cleavers, and the small elliptical blades regularly flaked on both surfaces, found in the campus site, do not occur at Dixthada" (Rainey 1939:388). The absence of such artifacts as copper tools suggested to Rainey that the Campus Site might be earlier than Dixthada, but he did not discount the possibility that differences between the assemblages might be the result of functional variability; he considered the Campus Site to be a temporary camp or workshop due to the absence of houses and midden deposits.

Rainey's (1939) paper, together with Nelson's (1937) article, have been referenced widely in subsequent archaeological studies. The excavations of the 1930s produced a large and varied collection of artifacts, including over 30 microblade cores which form the majority of the 45 specimens known to exist from the site. Much of the site remained undisturbed after the initial excavations from 1934 to 1936. Aerial photographs, including one taken by famed climber and photographer Bradford Washburn in 1938 during one of his many expeditions to Alaska (Roberts 1983), show the excavation area beyond the edge of a cultivated hayfield (Figures 3 and 4). Active interest in the site diminished for a number of years as the univer-

Figure 3. Aerial photograph of the Alaska Agricultural College and School of Mines, sometime between 1935 and 1937, showing excavation units in lower right (Otto Geist photograph #64-98-7366, Archives, Rasmuson Library, University of Alaska Fairbanks).

Figure 4. Aerial photograph by Bradford Washburn in 1938. It was published in the Letters to the Editor of *Life* magazine, January 9, 1939, along with the following caption: "I am enclosing two pictures which were made on Triple S Aero panchromatic film in Alaska last summer, while I was on an expedition for the National Geographic Society. The first picture shows Alaska College at Fairbanks: Flight altitude 300 ft. Exposure:1/225 sec. f:11 aero 2 filter. . . . The point which I thought might be of interest to you in these shots is the tremendous clarity of detail which I was able to obtain. This new film has been used for a year in miniature cameras, but these are some of the first pictures that have ever been taken with it in this large size." Excavation units show up clearly at lower right (Bradford Washburn photograph #2402, Boston Museum of Science).

sity campus continued to expand, although isolated tools were occasionally discovered elsewhere on the campus by J. Louis Giddings and others (and subsequently cataloged into the university museum collections in the 1950s). In his National Park Service-sponsored survey of Alaskan archaeological sites as potential National Historic Landmarks, Giddings (1962:159) considered the Campus Site for Landmark status, but dismissed it because "it appears to be nearly depleted."

The 1966 Salvage Excavations

In 1966, the University of Alaska, under President William R. Wood, announced the selection of the Campus Site locality as the location for a visitor's lookout—a platform featuring a large totem pole—to be adjacent to a campus perimeter road, sidewalks, and parking lot. Construction of the facilities threatened portions of the site,

prompting the initiation of an excavation program under the direction of Professor H. Morris Morgan of the Department of Anthropology and Geography, University of Alaska. Approximately 36 square meters were excavated to an average depth of 35 cm (Figure 5), resulting in the removal of about 15 cubic meters of soil. The site was excavated in units two meters on a side, working in five cm arbitrary levels (Hosley 1966), and over 4,000 artifacts were recovered by sifting the soil through ¼ inch mesh screen. An unpublished paper by Hosley and Mauger (1967) summarized the excavation, and field notes and photographs are on file at the University Museum in Fairbanks.

Observations made in 1966 confirm the lack of obvious stratigraphy noted in the 1930s. Beneath an uppermost dark organic soil 5–10 cm thick was an unstratified loess averaging 35 cm thick, darkening to a dark brown color from top to bottom. Downslope this loess lies directly on

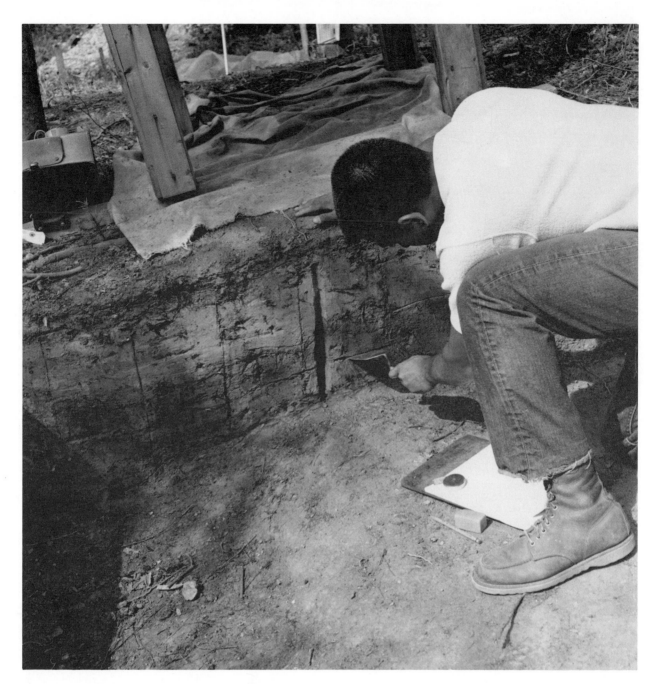

Figure 5. Excavation unit worked on by student Bill Hao in 1967, showing stratigraphic profile and lack of definite soil horizons (University of Alaska Museum photograph).

five feet of bedrock-derived schist rubble; nearer the crest of the hill the loess is separated from bedrock by a sterile yellow-buff sandy soil approximately five cm thick (Hosley and Mauger 1967:4). A "probable" fossil ice wedge observed in the sterile yellow-bluff soil did not extend up into the overlying loess.

Artifacts were found only in the loess, with the maximum density occurring midway within the stratum. The excavators noted that many artifacts were oriented in a vertical position in the matrix, suggesting a relatively dy-

namic soil matrix (Hosley and Mauger 1967:4). In some cases lithic artifacts were found close to nails and other recent debris.

The artifacts were classified into formal types and partially quantified (Table 3). Three relatively complete projectile points were recovered: a side-notched specimen, a "Lerma-like" point, and a third artifact "in every observable respect . . . a well-made Angostura point" (Hosley and Mauger 1967:9). Technological observations on artifacts relating to microblade production and burin manu-

Table 3. Partial artifact inventory from the 1966
excavations, from Hosley and Mauger (1967:6–9).

4 microblade cores
7 core tablets
276 microblades
3 notched burins
14 burin spalls
2 large blades
3 projectile points
2 large flake cores
scrapers and knives (uncounted)

facture were emphasized; microblade cores, microblades, burins, burin spalls, and macroblades were recognized. Raw materials noted in the assemblage were varieties of chert, and obsidian. Small amounts of charcoal and bone were collected.

Hosley and Mauger (1967:11–12) concluded that the Campus Site represented multiple components, citing the wide range of artifacts ("a core-and-blade industry, burins, lamelles, side-notched and lanceolate points"), variable degrees of skill in tool manufacture, and the

Figure 6. Dr. Edward Hosley (left) discusses the Campus Site with Dr. Hans-Georg Bandi (right) during excavations in 1967. Note totem pole and graded fill for the perimeter road, in the background (University of Alaska Museum photograph).

presence of 28 severely weathered flakes which contrasted with the lesser amount of patination on the rest of the assemblage. Technological similarities were noted between the Campus Site cores and specimens found in Band 8 at Onion Portage, Teklanika, and Anangula in the Aleutian Islands. Based on such comparisons, a maximum age for the microblade component was estimated at 5,500–6,500 B.C. (Hosley and Mauger 1967:12).

The 1967 Salvage Excavations

Appeals by Hosley to the University of Alaska for funding to preserve or study the Campus Site continued to go unheard. With funds provided by the Canadian Museum of Civilization, Edward Hosley continued salvage excavations at the Campus Site in 1967 (Figures 6 and 7). According to the field report (Hosley 1968:1), approximately 30 square meters were excavated to an average depth of

Figure 7. Bill Hao and Michael Aamodt laying out excavation units, looking northwest. Note Bunnell Building in the background, and covering vegetation (University of Alaska Museum photograph).

Figure 8. Sloping surface of the Campus Site during excavations of 1967, looking southeast over the Chena River/Tanana River floodplain in the background. Bill Hao and Ken Humphreys excavating (University of Alaska Museum photograph).

40 cm, inexplicably yielding 40 cubic meters of excavated matrix. Some backdirt from the 1930s excavations was also screened.

A map was prepared which locates the site perimeter and excavation limits. Some of the boundaries are problematic, however, as no criteria are given for the definition of site limits, and the configuration of the 1930s excavations does not match that shown in the aerial photographs (Figures 3 and 4). The more than 5,000 artifacts recov-

ered, when compared with a revised excavated matrix volume of 12 square meters, yield an average artifact density of 418 artifacts per cubic meter. All matrix was screened through ¼ inch mesh and selectively screened again through ⅛ inch mesh (Figure 8).

No cultural features were discovered in the 1967 excavations. Hosley (1968:2) states that "a number" of fossil ice wedges were identified by Troy Péwé, but it is not clear whether they were directly in the site or on nearby grounds of the university campus (Péwé 1965b:13). Ice wedges, together with a high frequency of vertically oriented artifacts in the site, would suggest solifluction as a significant soil process operating at the site. Variability in soil color was noted in the matrix—termed a "massive unbedded loess"—but was stated to be the result of neither stratification nor soil horizons (Hosley 1968:2). Small erosional channels with irregular loess infillings were detected within the body of the primary loess deposit.

The artifacts recovered were not quantified, but included "waste flakes. . . . Campus cores and core fragments, Campus 'notched' burins, other burin types, burin spalls, projectile points and fragments of these, core tablets [i.e. platform rejuvenation flakes], knives, scrapers [predominantly end scrapers], large numbers of microblades and fragments, and scattered organic materials" (Hosley 1968:2). The latter were said to be "finely divided" and insufficient for radiocarbon dating. There was

observed a tendency for cores, microblades, and small end scrapers to be more common in the upper portion of the deposit, while burins and projectile points were more common deeper in the deposit. A popular, illustrated account of the 1967 excavations was published in the university yearbook of 1968 (Aamodt et al. 1968).

The 1971 Excavations

In 1971 the Campus Site locale looked much as it does today, as construction was completed on the road, sidewalks, and parking lot, and the totem pole was installed (Figure 9). A group of university students under the direction of Dr. John Cook again excavated portions of the site. In late May, and again in August, six one-meter square units were opened. The purpose was twofold: to teach excavation techniques and to determine whether any archaeological material remained in place at the Campus Site.

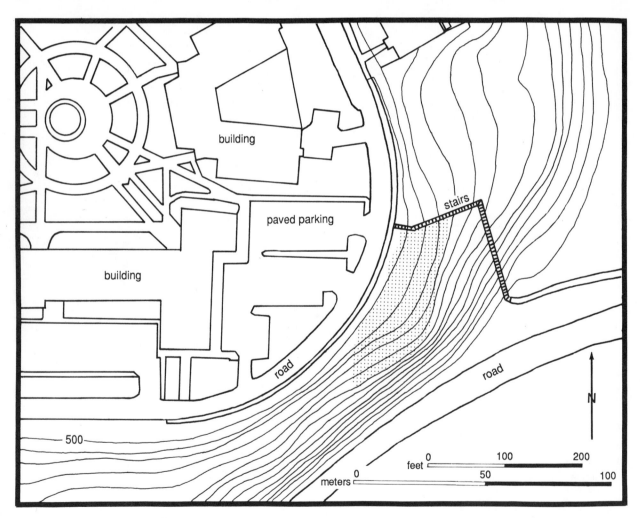

Figure 9. Map of the Campus Site, showing topography and modern facilities (from university facility engineering maps). Approximate portion of the original site surface remaining is stippled. Contour interval is five feet.

Figure 10. The campus of the University of Alaska Fairbanks, as it looked about 1980. Note totem pole in lower center. (Sabra McCracken photograph, University of Alaska Fairbanks).

The exact location of all six units is not clear, although a set of excavation notes is on file with the collection. A new coordinate system for designating units was employed, unrelated to that used in 1966 and 1967. In several instances the excavators encountered soft fill and recent debris indicating previously excavated areas. Nonetheless, stone artifacts were collected, and at least one thin carbonaceous lens was observed to indicate undisturbed prehistoric deposits. Each artifact was measured in place, and screens were not used.

The 110 specimens recovered in 1971 did not expand the range of known artifact forms from the Campus Site, although they constituted a welcome increase to the overall sample size. Flakes and microblades form most of the collection. The project was successful in demonstrating that prehistoric cultural material remained at the Campus Site, in apparently undisturbed contexts, despite the many different excavations and the university improvements.

Current Status of the Site

For almost twenty years after the development of the 1960s, the Campus Site was undisturbed (Figure 10). The totem pole was removed in 1987. Spruce and birch trees grace the slope, and several informal paths wind among the grass and bushes. Several shallow meter-square depressions can be discerned, probably from the 1971 excavations. Graders pushing snow off the campus perimeter road upslope occasionally scatter gravel across part of the site. There is little surface soil exposure, but artifacts can still be scuffed up here and there. A note filed with the University of Alaska-Fairbanks collection, signed by David Plaskett and pertaining to artifacts #75–6001 to 75–6009, reads "collected over the edge of bluff near totem pole and directly above the highway . . . in same location in 1973, 1974, 1975." Judging from the excavation patterns of the past and the recovery of additional artifacts in the 1970s in controlled and uncontrolled circumstances, it is likely that intact Campus Site deposits remain.

THE CAMPUS SITE COLLECTIONS

Artifacts and supporting documentation from the Campus Site excavations have resided in several different museums since the original discovery in 1933. Soon after the Campus Site was discovered on the grounds of the Alaska Agricultural College and School of Mines, the institution evolved into the University of Alaska (Keim 1969:233). The artifacts were the responsibility of members of the faculty (primarily Froelich Rainey). A *de facto* museum was administered by Otto Geist, a self-trained paleontologist/archaeologist/naturalist and all-around collector at the university (Keim 1969). The institution was gradually formalized and developed over the decades, until now a large modern museum building with public displays and curation and research facilities forms a major element of the University of Alaska Fairbanks. Despite numerous moves and countless handlings by professionals and students, the Campus Site material from the 1930s seems to have suffered remarkably little attrition. It would appear that some specimens were lost (Bandi and West n.d.:2), but the microblade cores—always considered the showpieces of the collection—are accounted for.

That is not to say that all the 1930s material is uniformly accessible, as loans and trades of specimens with other institutions broke up the original collection. A common practice of the 1930s was to trade small type collections among museums so that each institution had a broader representative sample of archaeological and ethnological material (Cole 1985:244–279), and this policy is responsible for connections with institutions in Tucson (Arizona), Moscow (U.S.S.R.), and Copenhagen (Denmark). Sponsorship of the early excavations by the American Museum of Natural History, and the availability of knowledgable review by Nels Nelson, prompted the shipment of artifacts to New York. For this restudy collections were acquired from the University of Alaska Museum, the Canadian Museum of Civilization in Quebec, Canada, and the Arizona State Museum in Tucson. Copies of correspondence exist to suggest that three other institutions have or have had additional Campus Site material: the American Museum of Natural History in New York, the National Museum in Copenhagen, Denmark, and the University of Moscow, U.S.S.R.

The University of Alaska Museum

The University of Alaska Museum in Fairbanks holds Campus Site material collected in the 1930s and material from more recent excavations. The investigations of 1966 were conducted under the auspices of the Department of Anthropology and Geography at the University of Alaska, and consequently the University of Alaska Museum retained all the resulting specimens. For the same reason, artifacts discovered in 1971 were accessioned by the University Museum. The institution's overall holdings—according to their tabulations of 1977—consist of 676 specimens excavated between 1933–1937 (cataloged as "CS-3-specimen number"), 4,212 specimens excavated in 1966 (cataloged as "CS-66-specimen number"), and 110 specimens recovered in 1971 (cataloged as "CS-71-specimen number"). The exact number of artifacts in the collections differs according to the assumptions made, however, because some accession numbers represent flake lots rather than individual specimens, and uncataloged and unlabeled artifacts are also present in the collection. Nonetheless, the Fairbanks sample is the largest Campus Site collection available, and contains the largest number of microblade cores and burins. This undoubtedly reflects recovery and collecting bias from procedures used in the 1930s work.

Probably in part because of the size and history of the University of Alaska Museum sample, there is much variability in the curation and packaging methods used for the collection. The museum has a large compactor system for storing collections efficiently, easing accessibility. But the specimens—especially the 1930s material—are stored in a hodge-podge of 35 mm film cannisters, glass jars, specimen vials, specimen boxes, envelopes, and cigar boxes. For the lithic material the packaging manner is not too critical, although two cigar boxes of large uncataloged flakes were excluded from the present analysis because their origin was dubious. The few faunal remains seem to have suffered little damage or loss from the packaging method, either. Perhaps the most potentially detrimental effects of the curation have been on charcoal samples intended for radiocarbon dating. Some were placed directly into cardboard photographic slide containers and sealed shut with tape, while others were inserted directly into metal film cannisters. Such handling may or may not have any effect on radiocarbon assay of the samples, but the facts bear mention to assist other researchers in evaluating the credibility of the reported radiocarbon dates.

The notes and other records accompanying the artifacts are another important part of the Campus Site collections.

No documentation, except for the published reports, exists in the museum's files from the 1930s work. Notes, artifact catalogs, and photographs from the 1966 excavations are on file, although no site map was produced beyond the sketch by Hosley (1968) used as the basis for Figure 42. The notes and artifact catalogs from both the 1966 and 1967 excavations are cross-filed so both the University of Alaska Museum and the Canadian Museum of Civilization have a complete set. The documentation for the 1971 excavations, on file in Fairbanks, consists of almost a dozen pages of student field notes.

The American Museum of Natural History, New York

The artifacts collected from the Campus Site in 1934 and 1935 were sent to Childs Frick of the American Museum of Natural History, for subsequent scrutiny by Nels Nelson. Likely the archaeological material was treated much like the paleontological material recovered at the time, for which "because the college lacked storage space and the American Museum wanted the specimens, an arrangement eventually was worked out whereby they would be sent to New York for study and the college could request the return of many of them when space became available to house them properly" (Keim 1969:215–216). In September of 1937 Froelich Rainey wrote from Fairbanks that "last spring the entire archaeological collection from the college campus site was returned to us here at the University from the American Museum." Nonetheless, some confusion existed as to whether all the material from the Campus Site was returned, and a personal inquiry in May of 1945 by Charles E. Bunnell, then president of the University of Alaska, was answered by H. L. Shapiro of the American Museum of Natural History to the effect that Dr. Nelson had returned all specimens.

Yet the idea that the American Museum of Natural History held Campus Site artifacts persisted into the following two decades. In his discussion of burins from the Campus Site, Irving (1955:380), states that "a small type collection is at the American Museum of Natural History; the rest of the material is now in the Museum of the University of Alaska." Returning from the Society for American Archaeology Annual Meeting held in Ann Arbor in 1967, where he presented a joint paper (with Jeffrey Mauger) on the 1966 excavations, Edward Hosley wrote in a memorandum to department chairman Erna Gunther that "Richard Woodbury said that he knows of a small collection of Campus Site materials at the AMNH . . .". Mauger (1970:7) also referred to the collection. In 1977 David C. Plaskett corresponded with the American Museum of Natural History, requesting information about the possibility of Campus Site artifacts there. Some correspondance about the Campus Site between Froelich Rainey and Clark

Wissler, and Rainey and Nels Nelson, was found in New York by museum staff, but Nelson's files and other pertinent records were not thoroughly searched. No accession numbers for Campus Site specimens were recorded at the museum in New York.

Again, as part of this restudy, a written request was made to the American Museum of Natural History for any information concerning the possibility of Campus Site material there. In looking into the matter, staff members found no record of Campus Site collections remaining at the American Museum of Natural History, although the Department of Paleontology discovered a detailed list, notes by Nelson, field notes of Jack Dorsh, and other documents concerning the Campus Site. Unfortunately, museum staff could research no further, and the author had no opportunity to travel and inspect the records first-hand in New York. Thus there is still the chance that additional unaccessioned Campus Site artifacts, or useful records, may be researched at the American Museum of Natural History.

Arizona State Museum, Tucson

The Arizona State Museum in Tucson (affiliated with the University of Arizona) holds six Campus Site artifacts. Documentation for them is sparse, although their catalog numbers (1937/specimen number) imply that they were obtained from the 1937 excavations (one artifact, a biface with catalog number #11–2635, is illustrated in Rainey's 1939 article). A two-page record on file with the notes in Fairbanks, entitled "Permanent Loan Collection to the Arizona State Museum," indicates that the six specimens were sent to Tucson along with archaeological material from St. Lawrence Island, the Punuk Islands, and Point Hope (all in Alaska). The Arizona State Museum Campus Site collection consists of one microblade core (Figure 12, a), two bifaces (Figure 26, e,), two retouched specimens, and a microblade. It is likely that Southwestern (U.S.) archaeological material was provided to the University of Alaska Museum in return, but no records have been found to confirm it. The six specimens were acquired on loan for this restudy project, individually wrapped in tissue and plastic bags.

The University of Moscow, U.S.S.R.

In 1938, in hope "that it will encourage your institute to co-operate with us in Bering Sea research," Froelich Rainey of the University of Alaska shipped to a Professor Plesievsky at the First University of Moscow a number of archaeological specimens from St. Lawrence Island and the Campus Site. A follow-up letter by Rainey in 1939 indicates that there was concern as to whether the shipment reached its destination, but some years later the issue was resolved. Rainey met Plesievsky again in 1957 when Rainey lectured at the Academy of Sciences in Moscow (their first meeting occurred in 1938, when—through arrangements made by then-Governor Ernest Gruening—Rainey went to Moscow to work out details of an unconsummated joint American/Soviet archaeological project in the Bering Straits region). The collection had been offloaded from a ship at Belfast, Ireland, and spent the duration of World War II there before it was forwarded to Moscow. The artifacts arrived intact, but a bottle of Scotch whiskey that Rainey had included and jokingly labeled "specimen of trade goods" was missing its original contents.

Recent efforts to correspond with Soviet officials regarding the status of the Campus Site materials sent to Moscow in 1938 have brought no response. At the request of the author, James VanStone inquired about the matter when he visited the Soviet Union in the early 1980s, but received no information. Another inquiry in 1987 was forwarded to Soviet ambassador Yuri Dubinin personally by Archibald Roosevelt III, with no results. For the purposes of this restudy, any useful information on the Moscow collection must be gleaned from the shipping list, which has survived in the Fairbanks records.

The 22 Campus Site artifacts sent to Moscow in 1938 were listed individually, with consecutive catalog numbers of U-1 through U-22. It is not difficult to visualize some of them from the descriptions entered on the shipping invoice (Table 4). Prismatic flakes probably refer to microblades, polyhedral cores are microblade cores, end-scrapers are flakes with steep retouch on their short axis, side-scrapers are flakes with steep retouch on their long axis, and leaf shaped blades are distinctively symmetrical lanceolate points similar to Specimen CS3–54 (Figure 26, f).

The National Museum, Copenhagen

Correspondence in 1938 between Froelich Rainey and Kaj Birket-Smith indicates that interest was strong in exchanging type collections of archaeological and ethnological materials between the Fairbanks and Copenhagen institutions. It was planned that specimens from St. Law-

Table 4. List of 22 Campus Site specimens sent to the University of Moscow in 1938, using original terms from the shipping invoice.

6 Prismatic flake struck from Polyhedral core
3 Polyhedral core
2 Retouched flake
1 Retouched blade
4 End-scraper
1 Side-scraper
1 Stone blade
2 Leaf shaped blade
1 Utilized Obsidian flake
1 Rough flake

rence Island and the Campus Site be traded for Danish "kitchen midden" material. However, Rainey wrote to Birket-Smith in December of 1938 that delays in illustrating and describing the Campus Site artifacts prevented shipment at that time, and suggested that the exchange be made "at a later date." An inquiry made to the Nationalmuseet in 1982 by the author was answered by Helge Larson, who stated that no Campus Site specimens were held by the Danish museum. Likely the planned exchange was preempted by World War II.

The Canadian Museum of Civilization, Quebec

Excavations at the Campus Site in 1967 were funded by the National Museum of Man, Ottawa (now the Canadian Museum of Civilization, Quebec), and consequently they retained the collections. The fieldwork that year followed closely the approach used in 1966, and the artifact and document collections are very similar. A total of 4,210 accession numbers were assigned to the 1967 collections, using the same catalog format as that used the prior year (CS-67-specimen number). Several microblade cores are included in the Canadian collection. Almost all the material is curated in plastic vials of uniform size, with cotton packing to prevent movement of specimens. Field notes accompany the 1967 Campus Site collection, as do photographs, but the latter were not procured for the restudy. A catalog of artifacts and their accession numbers was produced, but again, no field map is available.

METHODS USED IN THE CAMPUS SITE RESTUDY PROJECT

A combination of historic research and conventional archaeological analysis was used in the restudy. Details of illustration, photography, dating, and artifact description are presented in the following pages, with special attention to the definitions used in the lithic analysis. Archival work and correspondence with individuals, using methods of historical research, were necessary to reconstruct the excavation history of the Campus Site.

Obtaining the Historical Background

The discovery and early excavation of the Campus Site in the 1930s involved young students who remembered the experience as this volume was written. They graciously offered supplemental information to the known documentation on the early work. No field maps, notes, or photographs were filed with the collection at the University of Alaska Museum, although carbon copies exist of correspondence about exchanges of collections with other museums. Published articles by Dorsh (*Farthest North Collegian* 1934), Nelson (1935, 1937) and Rainey (1939, 1940) mention excavation details considered important at the time.

With the aid of an adept University of Alaska Fairbanks alumni office, individuals involved with the early excavations were contacted in hope of gaining new information and insights into the work of the 1930s. Froelich Rainey, now residing in Cornwall, England, provided comments through correspondance and conversations in 1982 when he returned to Fairbanks to give the keynote address at the annual meeting of the Alaska Anthropological Association. Three of the four individuals involved with the early excavations sponsored by the American Museum of Natural History—Albert Dickey, Walter Sullivan, and Archibald Roosevelt, Jr.—proved lively correspondents who added much contextual information for the original excavations of the 1930s. The widow of John Dorsh—Mrs. Bertha Dorsh—provided his original leather-bound field notebooks of 1933 and 1935, containing references to the team's excavations at the Campus Site. These people provided photographs of the excavators. A very useful acquisition was an aerial photograph of the university grounds showing the early excavation trenches at the

Campus Site, taken by Bradford Washburn during his pioneering aerial photography expeditions in Alaska (Roberts 1983). Review by Rainey, Dickey, Sullivan, and Roosevelt of partial draft manuscripts added details and helped strengthen the historical aspects of this volume. A similar chain of correspondence was necessary to track down the various existing and rumored Campus Site collections.

People involved in the later 1960s and 1971 excavations also provided personal notes and accounts of their work at the Campus Site. Many of them continue an academic interest in archaeology, and for them the Campus Site is one of the significant experiences contributing to their professional character. Interaction with the people who worked at the Campus Site or on its collections during the last 55 years was a rewarding aspect of the Campus Site restudy. Developing the historical perspective was sometimes a welcome contrast to the more conventional task of artifact description and illustration.

Obtaining the Collections

A total of three Campus site collections were obtained for the restudy; in each case the procedures for acquiring the material on loan were the same. The curating institution (University of Alaska Museum, Arizona State Museum, and Canadian Museum of Civilization) shipped the collection to the Department of Anthropology, University of Alaska Anchorage, where it was accepted by the author, who was then teaching there, and cosigned by Professor William B. Workman. The collections remained in the Anthropology laboratory of the university during the analysis, while the loan agreements were periodically extended over the next five years. Field notes, artifact catalogs, photography logs, and other documentation were also acquired with the artifact collections.

Dating Methods

Radiocarbon dating techniques were applied to one bone sample and several charcoal samples as part of the Campus Site restudy project. Efforts by Y. Katsui, John Cook, and Charles E. Holmes to use obsidian hydration dating on Campus Site specimens are summarized and compared to the radiocarbon dates. The results contrast with some temporal estimates of the Campus Site made on typological grounds. Details of the efforts to date the Campus Site, including the methods used, are presented later in this volume.

Faunal Analysis

Very little faunal material exists in the Campus Site collections. Most of the specimens consist of small calcined bone fragments no bigger than a cubic centimeter, making identification to species difficult. The faunal assemblage was inspected by John E. Lobdell, who proposed tentative evaluations to the extent that the sample allowed.

Artifact Illustration

Pen-and-ink drawings were selected over photography as the primary means of illustrating the Campus Site artifacts for two reasons. Given the predominance of chipped stone material in the collection, and the importance that has been placed on minute aspects of the microblade technology by other researchers, pen-and-ink is a preferred medium for showing important characteristics such as direction of flaking. Second, the illustrations are intended to be a visual catalog using a number of plates, and pen-and-ink was chosen over photography because it involves less expensive reproduction costs.

Pen-and-ink artifact illustrations were drawn by the author, with direction through the correspondence and detailed criticism of Lucile R. Addington; her excellent stylistic suggestions (Addington 1986) were always valued if not always followed. Because the plates were completed over the span of several years, they reflect an evolving personal illustration style which is evident in inconsistencies from plate to plate. A pencil was used under a bright light to draw each artifact to scale, showing the outline of the specimen and the intersection of all flake scars. A hand lens and calipers were used to maintain accuracy. The pencil sketch was then traced in ink on another sheet of paper, and finally the flake scars were shaded using a conventional technique. Pencil sketches of Campus Site microblade cores were graciously contributed by Shunichi Watanuki, who drew them in 1985 and 1986. These were useful for comparing perceptions of flake scar detail. Conventional symbols used in the illustrations include small dots to indicate areas of edge grinding, arrows to indicate location and direction of burin facets, and barred arrows to indicate the bulb of force on the ventral side of an illustrated specimen.

Photography

Historic photographic prints were obtained from individuals and institutions for use in this volume. Photographs of selected artifacts and artifact lots were taken for archival and publication use by the author, Michael Lewis, and other individuals.

Lithic Analysis

The attributes and techniques used in the analysis of the lithic artifacts from the Campus Site were chosen to provide a useful, balanced description of the several lithic technologies present in the assemblage. While artifact descriptions can be handled in a static framework, previous discussions of the Campus Site material—especially those pertaining to microblade production—have emphasized the manufacturing process as a potentially important diagnostic feature (Mauger 1971, Hayashi 1968). This is a useful emphasis for considering the microblade technology, as well as the macroblade, biface reduction, and core/flake technologies also present at the Campus Site.

All lithic artifacts, as well as specimens of organic and inorganic material, were entered as individual cases into the automatic data processing system of the University of Alaska by the author or Risa J. Carlson. Initially this work was done on a Honeywell computer, using both disc and tape files, but as that hardware became obsolete the data and programs were transferred to the university's VAX systems. Programming made use of the Statistical Package for the Social Sciences (SPSS), as updated (Nie et al. 1975; SPSS Inc. 1986). Most of the computerized data manipulation took place in Anchorage, but some was done through remote access in Fairbanks and Sitka.

Catalog numbers and spatial information are uniformly coded and formated in the initial columns for each artifact so that the entire collection can be manipulated simultaneously. The remaining columns were reserved for different attributes unique to subsets of the collection, such as bifaces, retouched specimens, microblades, bone lots, charcoal samples, etc. Over 9,000 cases were entered. An obvious discrepancy between this total and that obtained by adding the catalog entries of the three collections from different institutions reflects a combination of lost specimens not used in the computer analysis, and "new" (uncataloged) specimens which were assigned provisional numbers and entered into the data base.

THE ARTIFACTS

The artifact information is most useful to contemporary researchers interested in the Campus Site. This chapter presents qualitative and quantitative data for various artifact classes. The artifact typology was devised specifically to apply to the Campus Site material, with reference to common terms used in Alaskan archaeological analyses. Definitions of terms are provided in the text and in a glossary so that other researchers can make direct quantitative comparisons with other assemblages that may have been described using slightly different classification schemes. The artifact classes are organized and discussed according to the lithic technology that produced them. The four primary lithic technologies recognized in the assemblage are microblade production, macroblade production, biface reduction, and core-flake reduction. Secondary technological systems employed on products of these four primary technologies involve retouching and burination. A miscellaneous category includes ground stone tools and other items.

The total number of items coded in this analysis, including samples of bone, charcoal, and shell, is 9,226 (Table 5). This figure includes cataloged artifacts from the 1930s excavations, but excludes the cigar boxes of uncataloged lithic debris in the University of Alaska Museum collection because of questionable provenience. The total coded sample contains a disproportionately large number of formal tools, contributed by the selective recovery of the 1930s excavations. For meaningful quantitative comparisons, the 1930s material must be excluded, relying on the 1966, 1967, and 1971 samples to give a more balanced and accurate picture of the relative artifact frequencies to be found in the Campus Site artifact population.

Lithic Raw Materials

Although a variety of stone types were identified in the Campus Site collection by previous researchers (Nelson 1937, Rainey 1939, Hosley and Mauger 1967), for purposes of the restudy project they were reduced to five major materials: obsidian, chert, quartz, coarse material with conchoidal fracture, and coarse material with tabular fracture. Obsidian is a volcanic glass found in specific places in Alaska where igneous rocks are exposed in surface outcrops or alluvial/colluvial contexts, and—because of the regular rate at which a freshly flaked obsidian surface absorbs water—it can be chronometrically dated using the obsidian hydration method (Clark 1972, 1984a; Wheeler and Clark 1977; Michels 1984, 1985). Chert is a varicolored siliceous sedimentary rock which—in the Campus Site analysis—subsumes translucent and opaque materials that have been called jasper, moss agate, and flint. Quartz is a hard white igneous rock that supports conchoidal fracture, although it often contains severe fracture planes that limit its suitability for flaking. Materials grouped in the "coarse material with conchoidal fracture" category, of which there were just a few specimens, are made of homogenous igneous and metamorphic rocks. "Coarse material with tabular fracture" describes those few items of hard sedimentary or metamorphic rock that have bedding planes that redirect force vectors within them. Thermal alteration—sometimes called heat-treating when it is demonstrated to be culturally deliberate—of lithic materials was discriminated according to the commonly used criteria of thermal fracture planes, potlids, and reddish glossy discoloration (Crabtree and Butler 1964, Purdy and Brooks 1971, Mandeville and Flenniken 1974).

Microblade Technology

Although the microblade technology is only one of several stone-working techniques practiced by the prehistoric people at the Campus Site, it has received the greatest attention in the professional literature. This was an excusable response in the context of its initial discovery, since it was the similarity of the microblade cores to specimens found in the Gobi Desert of Mongolia that originally prompted important statements by Nelson (1935, 1937) and Rainey (1939) about Old and New World relationships. A fascination with microblade technology as a diagnostic temporal-cultural indicator for prehistoric cultures continued among practicing archaeologists in the Arctic and subarctic, so that several comparative studies have drawn upon the Campus site collections (Cook 1968; West 1967, 1981; Hayashi 1968; Morlan 1970). While these studies accurately describe many of the specimens, none was conducted with reference to the entire assemblage—that is, the combined collections from the University of Alaska Museum, the Canadian Museum of Civilization, and the Arizona State Museum. Thus the value of this comprehensive study is in part a repetition of the same observations on a larger sample size. In ad-

Table 5. Comparison of the combined 1966, 1967, and 1971 Campus Site samples (those recovered using systematic screening) with the total sample.

ARTIFACT CLASS	1966–1971 SAMPLE		TOTAL SAMPLE	
	Frequency	%	Frequency	%
Microblade Technology				
Microblade cores	9	.1	42	.4
Microblades	591	6.7	604	6.6
Initial spall	9	.1	9	.1
Trifaced ridge flake	0	0	1	< .1
Rejuvenation flake with blade face remnant	9	.1	20	.2
Rejuvenation flake with no blade face remnant	3	< .1	8	.1
Gull-wing flake	9	.1	15	.2
Macroblade Technology				
Macroblades	1	<.1	6	.1
Biface Technology				
Irregular biface	20	.2	40	.4
Battered biface	2	< .1	8	.1
Oval biface	3	< .1	5	.1
Triangular biface	2	< .1	4	< .1
Round basal fragment	1	< .1	9	.1
Square basal fragment	3	< .1	5	.1
Lanceolate point	2	< .1	7	.1
Biface tips	9	.1	16	.2
Notched point	1	< .1	2	< .1
Biface thinning flakes	427	4.9	468	4.9
Core/flake Technology				
Cores	8	.1	17	.2
Flakes	7,295	83.2	7,417	80.4
Nondiagnostic shatter	58	.7	69	.7
Retouched Specimens				
Retouched microblade	1	< .1	3	< .1
Retouched macroblade	1	< .1	6	.1
Flake: short axis retouch	18	.2	43	.5
Flake: long axis retouch	5	.1	13	.1
Flake: irregular retouch	20	.2	79	.8
Flake: misc. retouch	0	0	2	< .1
Burinated Specimens				
Donnelly burin	6	.1	22	.2
Flake: no platform preparation	3	< .1	4	< .1
Biface: platform preparation	1	< .1	3	< .1
Biface: no platform preparation	0	0	1	< .1
Retouch: platform preparation	0	0	1	< .1
Retouch: no platform preparation	0	0	1	< .1
Burin spall	6	.1	10	.1
Miscellaneous Stone				
Tabular slab	0	0	4	< .1
Unmodified cobble	1	< .1	6	.1
Hammerstone	0	0	4	< .1
Cobble Spall	2	< .1	3	< .1
Groundstone	1	< .1	3	< .1
Pebbles	39	.4	39	.4
Historic Trash	48	.5	48	.5
Charcoal Samples	102	1.2	102	1.1
Bone	38	.4	39	.4
Shell	18	.2	18	.2
TOTALS	8,781		9,226	

dition, observations are made that quantify certain attributes and relate them to a model of core preparation and microblade manufacture.

Such a model was developed by Mauger (1971) in detail, using the University of Alaska collection. Although unpublished, the study contains important observations on the microblade technology displayed at the Campus Site; this current analysis follows closely some of Mauger's perceptions. His characterization of the assemblage is largely qualitative, using a sample of 30 microblade cores and an unspecified number of microblades and debris from core preparation. The analysis which follows here quantifies the attributes that Mauger (1971) used to infer certain patterns in the microblade technology, and presents additional data with which to compare the Campus Site assemblage with material from other sites in the New and Old Worlds. An idealized microblade core, showing the parts of the core and the terms used to refer to them, is illustrated in the glossary of terms at the end of this volume.

Artifacts associated with microblade technology consist of microblades, the microblade cores from which they were derived, and certain classes of lithic debris resulting from microblade core preparation and maintenance. Other artifacts—such as pressure-flaking tools, hammerstones and abraders, and less distinctive lithic debris resulting from core preparation—are associated with the technology but cannot be easily discriminated from similar items related to other lithic technologies. The 42 microblade cores available from the Campus site constitute one of the largest samples from any single prehistoric site in Alaska. Discrete manufacturing stages identified in the microblade technology at the Campus Site consist of: (1) selection and general shaping of the core blank; (2) preparation of the platform; (3) preparation of the blade face; (4) removal of microblades; (5) platform rejuvenation; and (6) discard of the core. There may be occasional reversals of the order of platform and blade face preparation, but most of the artifacts—when they reflect the order—suggest the above sequence of events. The cores would seem to show no indication of subsequent use as hammerstones or wedges, although Cook (1968) interpreted some to have served a scraping function.

SELECTION AND GENERAL SHAPING OF THE CORE BLANK

The initial constraint on blank selection for microblade cores was the size and quality of the raw material. Most of the several different types of siliceous rock used can be unequivocally termed chert; no obsidian microblade core specimens are present in the collection. Few of the chert cobbles available locally in alluvial deposits of the Tanana River are larger than one's fist.

Beginning with a cobble, the knappers at the Campus Site had several options for creating a core from which microblades could be removed. In one unique case a cobble was split, and the fresh surface was used as a platform from which to remove microblades (Figure 11, c, d). A flake origin for one microblade core is confirmed by a positive bulb of force on one side (Figure 11, a), while 27 other specimens in the total core sample display enough of a positive flake scar forming one face to strongly suggest a flake origin; some examples have very little modification of the original flake blank's ventral surface (examples are Figures 11, e; 12, d; 13, c; 14, c; 19, b). Many of the remaining specimens exhibit on one face a centrally located facet of low relief that suggests, though not unequivocally, origin as a flake also (examples are Figures 11, f; 16, d;). While these centrally located facets may not be unambiguously identifiable as the remnants of a positive or negative flake scar, in most cases they display a plane and flake scar orientation indicating a flake detachment that must have occurred from a platform located some distance from the present perimeter of the specimen. In 13 instances flaking over most of the surface of both sides of the core has resulted in a bifacial appearance (examples are Figures 16, c; 17, b; 18, a). The core platforms on these bifacial specimens do not indicate whether they were formed by snapping a completed biface or by bifacially working a flake a little more extensively, although there are a few spalls resulting from platform preparation that suggest that some blanks were first flaked into bifaces.

Mauger (1971:5–6) considered all the microblade cores in his sample to have been made on flakes, citing remnants of the original flake's ventral surface in over half the cases, and a plano-convex cross-section as evidence for the remainder (Specimen CS67-4798 shown in Figure 11, d, which was made on a cortical cobble, was not included in the sample that Mauger analyzed). But a plano-convex cross-section may characterize a biface also, and thus does not necessarily confirm that all the cores originated as flakes.

There is no indication that any special sort of flake was selected as a blank for the intended microblade core. Obviously size must have been a criterion, and larger flakes were probably preferred. Microblade cores in the collection range from 0.8 g to 16.0 g in weight, giving some indication of the minimum size of the parent flakes.

Three of the 42 microblade cores show discoloration indicative of thermal alteration (Figure 15, d; 17, a; 19, b), although there is no indication as to when this occurred, or whether it was purposeful.

Shaping of the core blanks was accomplished through various degrees of bifacial or unifacial flaking, depending on the morphology of the parent flake. Smooth lateral sides and some cross-sectional symmetry were likely desired qualities at this stage of the manufacturing process.

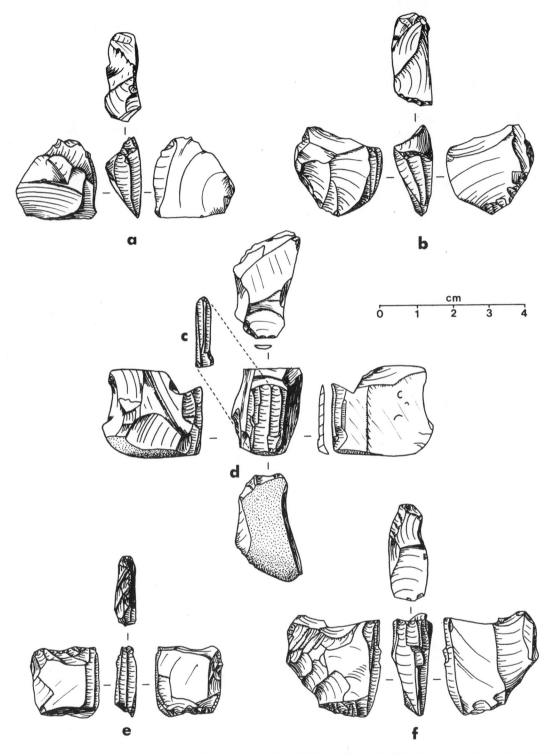

Figure 11. Microblade cores: a. (#67-2140), b. (#67-3125), d. (#67-4798), e. (#3-6), f. (#3-21); c. microblade (#67-2701) removed from Core #67-4798.

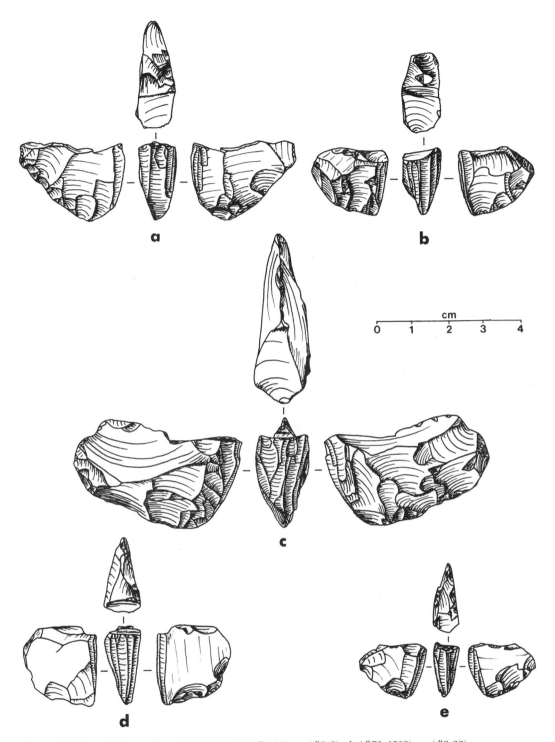

Figure 12. Microblade cores; a. (#A-12637), b. (#3-30), c. (#3-9), d. (#71-4233), e. (#3-33).

Subsequent blade face and platform preparation continued to alter the appearance of the blank, but final shaping of the keel may have been accomplished early in the development of the blank. The keels of the microblade cores in the sample are relatively straight, more or less parallel to the long axis of the specimen (and thus perpendicular to the blade face), with straight or gently curving profiles in plane view. In most specimens the keel displays many very small flake scars on both sides of the core, indicating abrasion and crushing. This has been interpreted by West (1967:368) as possibly due to contact with an anvil, as the core is vertically immobilized during blade manufacture. Mauger (1971:7–8) disagrees, citing his replicative experiments to suggest that the crushing is

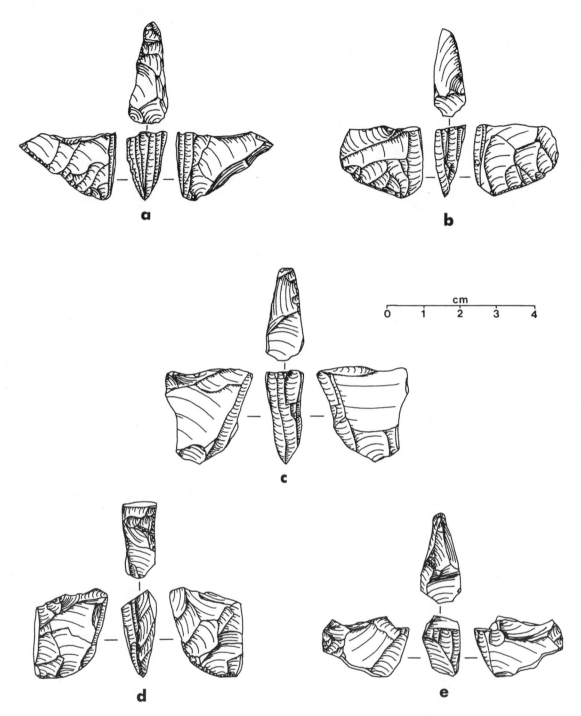

Figure 13. Microblade cores; a. (#3-14), b. (#3-10), c. (#3-32), d. (#3-64), e. (#3-18).

the result of either purposeful or inadvertent strengthening of the keel during initial shaping.

PREPARATION OF THE BLADE FACE

The methods used to prepare the initial blade face on the microblade core must be inferred from the lithic debris assemblage, since subsequent manufacture of microblades necessarily obliterates evidence on the core itself.

A relatively straight, narrow edge perpendicular to the keel was required to guide the first blade detachment. Such initial spalls identified in the Campus Site collection display unifacial and bifacial retouch (Figure 20, g–i), indicating that both flaking techniques were used to create the initial detachment of the blade face. Four bifacially worked examples and five unifacial examples constitute the sample. On the basis of size, these specimens are distinguished from a morphologically similar one (termed a

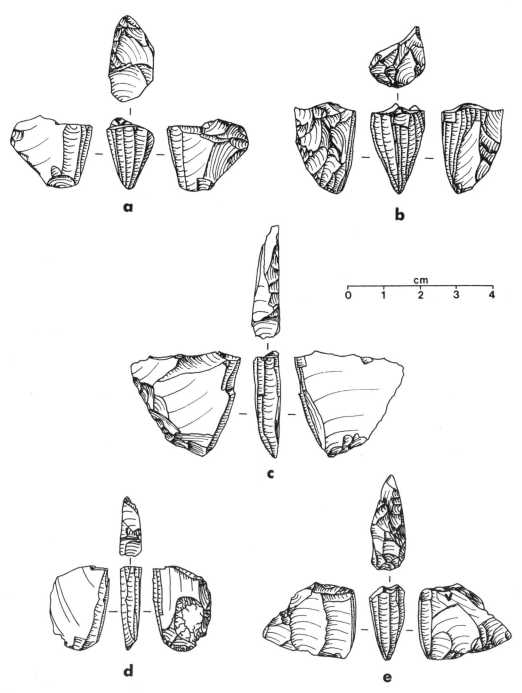

Figure 14. Microblade cores; a. (#3-29), b. (#3-13), c. (#3-4), d. (#3-7), e. (#3-27).

trifaced ridge flake) resulting from initial platform preparation (Figure 20, f). The initial blade face spalls are smaller in size than the single trifaced ridge flake identified, and are about the same size range as that of complete microblades (Table 6). One core (Figure 16, d) exhibits the remnant of a unifacially retouched edge on the blade face, but it appears to have been intended to realign an unsuitable arris formed by the lateral intersection of a prior blade scar with the side of the core. While it is not *initial* blade face preparation, it does verify that unifacial retouch was used to create straight ridges on the blade face to direct microblade removal.

PREPARATION OF THE PLATFORM

Techniques of platform preparation may be a diagnostic characteristic of microblade technologies, since there are several ways that the craftsman can create a plane

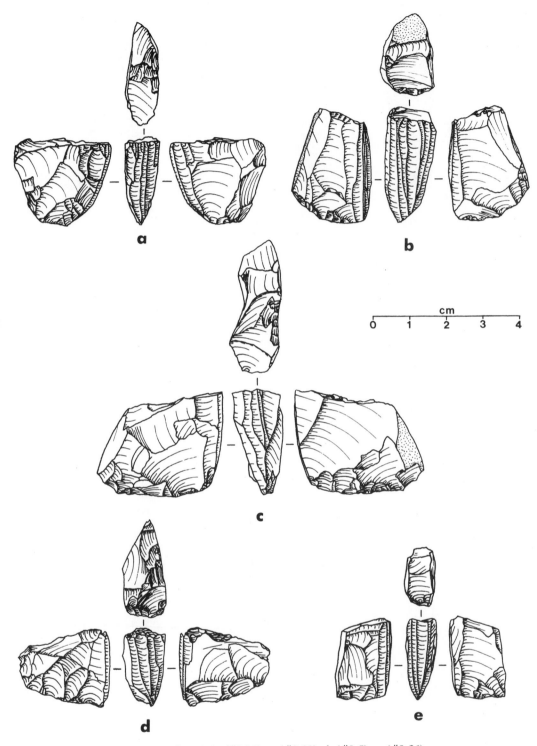

Figure 15. Microblade cores; a. (#3-19), b. (#3-12), c. (#3-31), d. (#3-5), e. (#3-26).

oriented perpendicular to the axis of the core. Two distinct approaches were used at the Campus Site, distinguished by the direction of flake removal. There is evidence to suggest that both of these methods were also used subsequently to rejuvenate the platform for continued microblade production.

One technique for creating the platform on the microblade core involved force directed from the side, perpendicular to the plane of the core. A flake was removed near the blade face end of the artifact, to produce a flake scar perpendicular to the blade face with one lateral margin feathering towards the blade face. A deep bulbar scar was

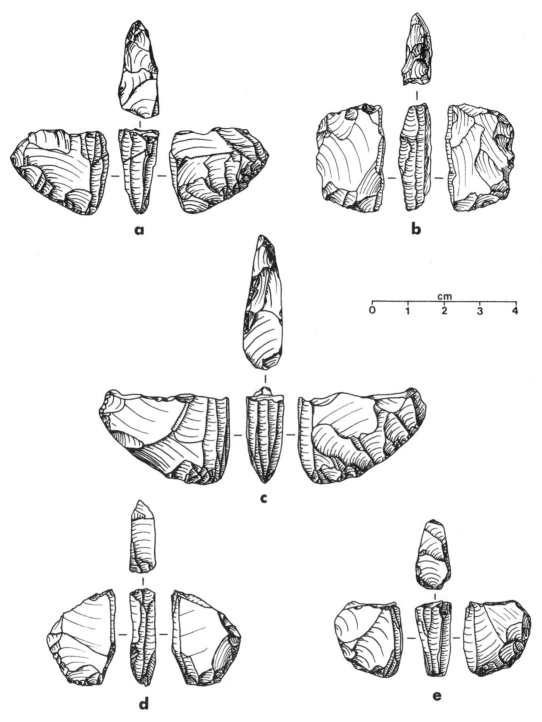

Figure 16. Microblade cores; a. (#67-1), b. (#3-17), c. (#3-16), d. (#3-25), e. (#3-28).

desired adjacent to the blade face to produce an angle between the scar and the blade face of less than 90 degrees. Experimentation by the author and others suggests that such an angle provides a better purchase for the punch or other pressure tool used for blade removal, compared to a perfectly flat surface oriented exactly 90 degrees to the blade face. The concavity of the platform surface was enhanced by subsequent flake removals, in which the point of pressure (or impact) was directly underneath that of the previous flake removal. Because the wave of force tends to parallel the surface contour, when succeeding flakes are removed with such aligned bulbs the concavity becomes more pronounced on the core, and distinctive flakes are produced in which the ventral and

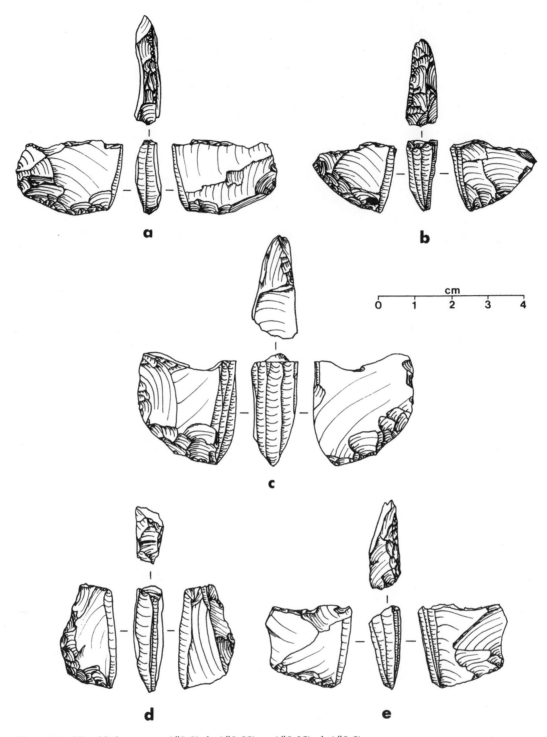

Figure 17. Microblade cores; a. (#3-1), b. (#3-22), c. (#3-15), d. (#3-2).

dorsal surfaces show extreme parallelism. In entirely different contexts, this successive alignment of bulbs is technologically similar to that of the Setouchi technique of Japan, although there the intent is to produce large symmetrical flakes with uniform and parallel dorsal and ventral surfaces, to be retouched into morphologically standardized implements (Morlan 1971:148–149).

Evidence in the Campus Site collections for this platform preparation technique consists of the flake debris produced, and of the negative scars remaining on the cores. Mauger (1971:9) terms the distinctive flakes "side struck platform flakes", referring to the fact that they are struck from the side of the core. When viewed in cross-section from the proximal end, the flakes take on the ap-

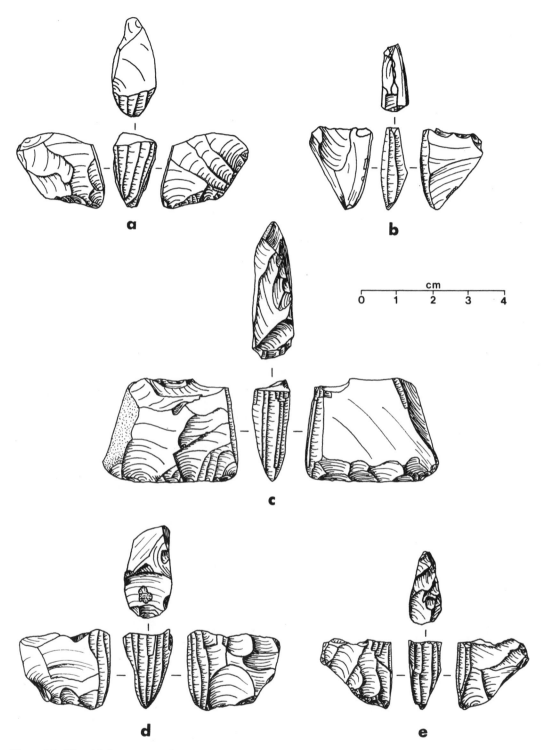

Figure 18. Microblade cores; a. (#66-418), b. (#66-1), c. (#3-2883), d. (#3-3015), e. (#3-23).

pearance of a "flying V", and are sometimes informally called "gull-wing flakes" by Alaskan archaeologists. Specimens can be singled out of the debris collection using the co-occurring criteria of: (1) width greater than length, (2) length not grossly exceeding maximum width of microblade cores, (3) positive bulb on the ventral sur-face aligned directly beneath the bulb of a negative scar that covers most of the dorsal surface, (4) lateral edges feather more or less symmetrically, and (5) distal dorsal surfaces often consist of a flat facet oriented with a high angle to the ventral surface—the facet representing a por-tion of the side of the core. Replicative experiments are

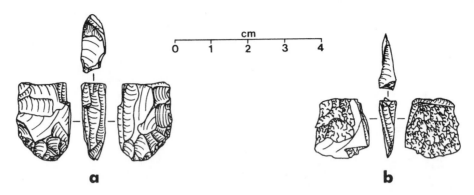

Figure 19. Microblade cores; a. (#3-36), b. (#3-3).

Table 6. Descriptive statistics for initial blade face spalls.

	Length (mm)	Width (mm)	Thickness (mm)	Weight (g)
Initial blade face spalls (N = 9)	23.2 mean	6.7 mean	3.8 mean	0.5 mean
	13.3 min	4.5 min	2.2 min	0.4 min
	31.5 max	11.7 max	5.7 max	0.8 max
	5.5 SD	2.2 SD	1.2 SD	0.1 SD

needed to determine to what extent this platform preparation technique consistently produces such flakes; it is likely that less distinctive flakes are also produced and discarded, to go unrecognized in the lithic debris assemblage. The five criteria mentioned here were applied rigorously to isolate such specimens in the Campus Site collections, with the realization that many more flakes actually produced in this manner can't be consistently discriminated. A total of 15 such specimens were identified.

A set of joining flakes in the Campus Site collection confirms that side-struck platform flakes sometimes exhibit less distinctive characteristics. Viewed individually, some but not all of the specimens would be unquestionably recognized as the result of microblade core platform preparation, using the five criteria mentioned above. When fitted together, however, five flakes provide instructive insight into the core preparation process. The five specimens, together with a sixth platform preparation flake, were apparently recovered during the 1966 excavations, although they have no catalog number. Mauger (1971:9) and Hosley and Mauger (1967:7) recognized these specimens and refer to them as fitting a microblade core recovered during the excavations of the 1930s. The material is a very dark grey chert with tiny tan inclusions throughout, and can thus be differentiated macroscopically from other raw materials. Nonetheless, and despite considerable effort on the part of the author and other colleagues who dropped into the laboratory from time to time during the restudy project, the sixth platform preparation flake (which is definitely of the same material) could not be fitted onto the five cojoining pieces, nor could these or

any other platform preparation flakes be fitted onto a microblade core in the Campus Site collections.

Preparation of the remainder of the core platform element, distant from the area immediately adjacent to the blade face, required no exaggerated concavity. Instead, overlapping flakes were struck or pressed off unidirectionally from the side of the core, to produce a plane ranging from perpendicular to oblique in relation to the plane of the core. The microblade cores in the collection show considerable variability in the portion of the platform distant from the blade face, and some specimens exhibit a ridge (Figure 12, c; 19, b). Flakes removed in preparing that portion of the core's platform are not so easily discriminated from the general lithic debris assemblage, since they do not necessarily show aligned bulbar scars or the "gull-wing" profile. They do display a width greater than length (and hence would be characterized as "side-struck" in some technical vocabularies), and are of a length comparable to the width of microblade cores. In some cases a set of negative flake scars (aligned with the direction of force responsible for the ventral surface of the flake) covers the proximal half of the dorsal surface, with a sudden change of angle at the midpoint of the flake's dorsal surface and a broad flat negative flake scar over the distal portion of the dorsal surface. This dorsal surface topography reflects the junction between the core's side and its previously worked core platform surface, the new platform preparation flake having removed a portion of both. While it is clear that microblade core platform preparation must have produced such flakes, and while it is equally clear that such flakes are present in the Campus Site collection, it is not easily ascertained to what extent

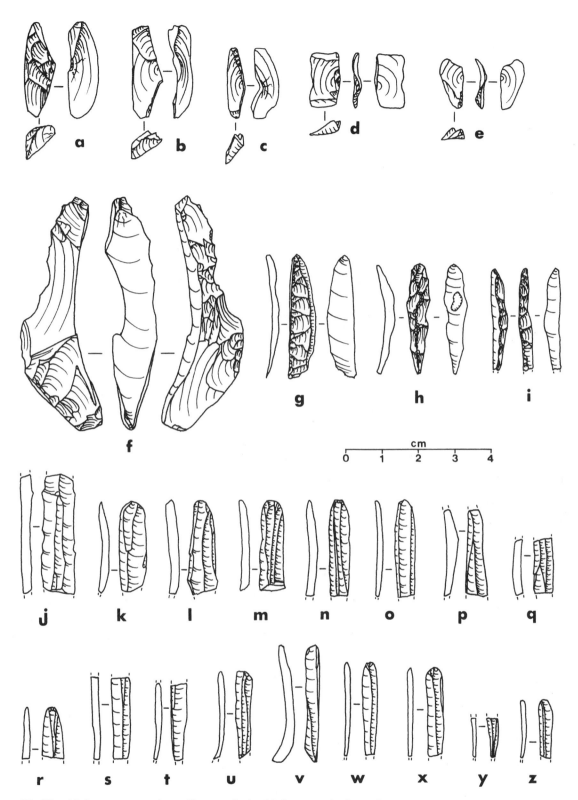

Figure 20. Microblade core preparation artifacts, and microblades; a.–e. "gull-wing" microblade core rejuvenation flakes (#67-8, #3-181, #66-1098, #67-3906, #67-4812), f. trifaced ridge flake (#3-382), g.–i. initial spalls from microblade core (#66-2887, #66-98, #66-1276), j.–z. microblades.

other lithic technologies—such as biface or core/flake reduction—might also occasionally produce flakes with such attributes. Experimentation, and detailed technological analyses of Alaskan assemblages reflecting strictly biface reduction or core/flake reduction, may help resolve the issue. In the collections assembled for this analysis, such specimens were not singled out from the flake assemblage.

There is some suggestion that core platform preparation done from the side of the specimens was done using an anvil to support the opposing side of the core, according to Mauger (1971:10–11). He cites as evidence the abrupt termination of the preparation flakes, in which the distal end of the negative flake scar may form a right angle with the side of the core. He also mentions crushing on the proximal end of the flake scars as indicative of anvil support, but qualifies the statement by saying that "the crushing may also stem from removing the lip created by the negative bulbs of stress" (Mauger 1971:10–11). Mauger's perceptions are valuable in that they reflect some "hands-on" experimentation, but no confirming replication has been attempted as part of this current study.

Another important observation by Mauger (1971:11), and one perhaps less controvertible than the issue of anvil support, concerns the side of the core from which this method of platform preparation was executed. While the knapper has his choice of either side of the core to flake from, Mauger notes that the right side of the core (using the orientation of the core illustrations in this study as reference for right and left) was preferred. In his sample of 30 microblade cores, he was able to characterize 16 as having platforms prepared from the right side, six with platforms prepared from the left side, and one with platform preparation flakes removed from both sides (the remainder of his sample was not described). With the larger sample used in this restudy, the specimens are differentiated into 25 with platforms prepared from the right side, 11 from the left side, two from both sides, one from the back of the core directed toward the blade face end, and three with no platform scars other than a single facet resulting from rejuvenation directed toward the blade face. No other reason than "habit" was suggested by Mauger for the right side preference, and it may reflect "handedness" in the sense of a preference for the right or left hand. There is precedent for such inferences made from archaeological data (Toth 1985), including the stone blade industry at Anangula in the Aleutian Islands of Alaska (Aigner and Fullem 1976:77–78).

While the preceding discussion has focused on one technique for microblade core platform preparation, involving force directed from the side, there is also some evidence to suggest that force directed from the blade face was also sometimes used to prepare the platform for initial microblade production. This involved removal of a long primary spall from one edge of the core, at a right angle to the intended blade face. Judging from the platforms on the microblade cores, this technique was rarely used, as only three specimens exhibit a flake scar attesting to force from the blade face that removed the entire upper edge of the artifact, and it is not clear whether the removal occurred at the initial stages of core preparation or during later platform rejuvenation.

A single artifact (Figure 20, f) in the Campus Site collection is comparable to the initial spall produced by the Yubetsu technique used to prepare microblade cores at the Shirataki Site in Japan (Morlan 1967:177), and which Kobayashi (1970) calls a trifaced ridge flake. The specimen has a triangular cross section formed by two flaked facets comprising the dorsal surface, with the third side consisting of the flake's ventral surface. The longitudinal ridge on the dorsal surface was formed through bifacial flaking of the intended core, prior to detachment of the trifaced ridge flake. The platform on the spall consisted of a flat facet adjacent to a bifacially flaked ridge reflecting the former bifacial edge of the core. There is considerable abrasion on the platform ridge, presumably to blunt the edge and prepare it for removal of the spall. Subsequent spalls removed from the specimen using the same platform would have produced long, narrow specimens with a rectangular cross-section, sometimes termed "ski-spalls" (Morlan 1967:177). Ski-spalls are not present in the Campus Site collection, and thus their production in the microblade technology is not suggested. Instead, removal of the tri-faced ridge flake must have been followed immediately by microblade production. Such a procedure would correspond to "manufacturing sub-system A2" in Kobayashi's (1970:39–40) model of microblade industries in Japanese prehistory.

MICROBLADE MANUFACTURE

In this analysis the beginning of microblade manufacture is taken to be the stage where prismatic blades are removed, the blades having a dorsal surface formed by parallel longitudinal flake scars. This definition is arbitrary in some ways, as it excludes the removal of initial spalls discussed earlier as part of blade face preparation. Mauger (1971:12–14) suggests that the initial spall on Campus Site microblade cores may have been removed from the intended blade face either before or after preparation of the platform. The single trifaced ridge flake in the collection (CS3-382, the only artifact indicating initial core platform preparation using force directed at the blade face), displays a facet at the platform which apparently reflects a single spall removed perpendicular to the force that removed the trifaced ridge flake itself. Although this evidence is tenuous, the artifact implies that the initial spall was removed prior to preparing the core's platform, and thus removal of the initial spall was included under the heading of blade face preparation in this analysis.

The sequencing of subsequent spall removals on the blade face remains somewhat ambiguous as well, and secondary spall removals from the blade face may have occurred either before or after preparation of the core's platform. These secondary spalls are triangular in cross section, consisting of the ventral surface of the spall, a portion of the negative flake scar left from removal of the initial spall, and a multiple-faceted surface reflecting a portion of the side of the core. Descriptive terms for these artifacts vary, with "secondary spall" favored by Mauger (1971:13), "secondary ridge flakes" used by Sanger (1968a:198), and "corner platform spalls" used by Hadleigh-West (1967:369). Such specimens were noted in the collection, but were not quantified separately from the remainder of the microblade assemblage. Secondary spalls need not be produced only immediately after removal of the primary spall, since lateral expansion of the blade face at any point in the production process may produce specimens displaying a negative blade scar and a portion of the core's side as the dorsal surface of the spall.

The force used to remove microblades from a core is generally thought to be applied through indirect percussion or pressure (Mauger 1971:14–15; Sheets and Muto 1972; Hadleigh-West 1967:368). The latter is favored as an explanation by Mauger (1971:14–15), based on the small size and regularity of the microblades, small size of the blade platforms, lack of rings and undulations on the ventral surface of microblades, and his first-hand experimentation and replication of microblades using various percussion and pressure techniques. Mauger (1971:16) cites Bordes and Crabtree (1969:9–10) to suggest that "the straightness of the microblades in the Campus collection and their corresponding facets on the cores suggests that during blade removal the bases of Campus cores were supported." Small step fractures and abrasion on the bases of some microblade core specimens from the Campus Site have been attributed to contact with an "anvil" or other hard surface during blade removal (Hadleigh-West 1967:368). Del Bene (1978:11) even suggests that the basal damage is definite but slight enough to imply that "the core might have been shielded from full contact with a resistant material by the interposition of a resilient material."

In addition to basal support for the keel of the microblade core, some lateral support during microblade manufacture is also likely. The mechanism suggested by Hadleigh-West (1967:368) was judged unworkable by Mauger (1971:16), who attempted to replicate it. However, experimentation by the author and others indicates that some sort of vice arrangement is certainly helpful, if not necessary, in replicating microblade cores and microblades. Wear on some of the core specimens further

supports hypothesized use of a vise. Cook's (1968:124–127) discussion of wear on Campus Site cores is not pertinent in this context, since he was concerned with modification to core platforms as a result of use. But polish on the sides of some core specimens in the Campus Site collections has also been observed by Del Bene (1978:11–13, 1980) and Mauger (1971:16). The latter author was reluctant to interpret such lateral polish on the microblade cores as the result of vice wear, since it was not produced in his replicative experiments. However, Del Bene (1980:34–35), generalizing about his analysis of microblade cores from the Campus Site as well as the sites of Dixthada, Healy Lake, and Dry Creek, identified wear on the sides of the core as due to resistant materials and wear on the platforms and keels to be from resilient materials:

> I feel that this complex of damages is indicative of the employment of a holding device during the process of blade manufacture. In some instances a shallow groove has been worn into the facial areas; this provides more information concerning the precise shape and limits of the contact between the holding device and the core. . . . the device probably possessed two short arms which contacted the core faces. The cores would seem to have have been held in place by lashing them tightly into the slot by wrapping with some cordage. This would explain the resilient damage found on the platform area, and for that matter upon the dorsal surfaces of the platform tablets. If the base and keel were shaped to fit the slot in the device well, this simple system of lashing would be quite efficient.

Localized preparation of the platform and the blade face for removal of each individual microblade is evident in the Campus Site assemblage. The negative bulbs left on the core blade face by removal of each microblade had to be modified before subsequent blade removal, because the overhanging lip was not usually strong enough to support the force necessary to remove another microblade. In removing this overhang, the proximal dorsal surface of the impending microblade was realigned to better guide subsequent blade removal. Tiny flakes were chipped off the core's blade face to do this, using the core platform as a purchase for the flaking instrument. The flaking done to realign arrises on the dorsal surface of the pending microblade also served to isolate and better define the platform, so that the resulting microblades consistently display relatively small platforms.

The metric and discrete attributes of microblades form a useful array of data for regional comparisons of prehistoric technology (Anderson 1970:8–9; Sanger 1968b:114–115, 1970; Wyatt 1970; Holmes 1986:137), and samples of Campus Site microblades have been described in this context (Irving 1953:62–63; Cook 1968:121–123, Owen 1988). It is useful to summarize

Table 7. Descriptive statistics for the microblades.

	Length (mm)	Width (mm)	Thickness (mm)	Weight (g)
Microblades:	–	4.9 mean	1.5 mean	0.2 mean
including	–	2.0 min	0.5 min	0.1 min
fragments	–	14.0 max	7.4 max	3.0 max
(N = 604)	–	1.5 SD	0.6 SD	0.2 SD
Complete	16.3 mean	5.8 mean	1.9 mean	0.3 mean
microblades	7.8 min	2.5 min	0.8 min	0.1 min
(N = 39)	42.8 max	14.0 max	7.4 max	3.0 max
	8.4 SD	2.5 SD	1.1 SD	0.5 SD

this information again, for subsequent comparative analyses, using the larger Campus Site sample now available. Continuous variables are described for complete microblades alone, as well as the entire collection (Table 7). A very conservative definition was taken to discriminate complete microblades, requiring not only the termination of the distal end to be discernible but also all of the platform on the proximal end; specimens were not termed complete if the platform was crushed. Only 39 complete microblades were recovered, and the majority of the microblade collection consists of broken specimens: 216 proximal fragments, 254 medial fragments, and 95 distal fragments. One obsidian specimen stands out among the otherwise chert microblade assemblage. Forty-four, or 7.3% of the microblades, are thermally altered. Triangular cross sections are evident on 169 (28%) of the microblades, while the remainder have three or more dorsal blade scars producing a trapezoidal or polyhedral cross section. The thickness measurement is a maximum for the microblade overall, and was not necessarily taken just below the bulb of force as suggested by Sanger et al. (1970:115), or as suggested by Cook (1968:121).

PLATFORM REJUVENATION

As microblades were removed from the core, the platform morphology gradually changed until it no longer was suitable for microblade removal. Improper platform angle was one circumstance warranting rejuvenation, judging from the rejuvenation spalls noted in the Campus Site assemblage, as was improper platform morphology. Flakes were removed from the core platform to make it again suitable for microblade removal. The technological options parallel those for the original core platform preparation, and force was applied either from the blade face or from the side of the core to remove material from the platform and rejuvenate the core. The two sources of information about platform rejuvenation techniques are the negative flake scars on the microblade core platforms, and the rejuvenation flakes themselves.

Rejuvenation flakes and the negative flake scars on the microblade core platforms both unambiguously attest to

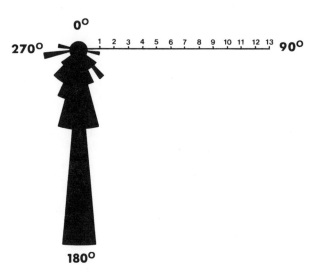

Figure 21. Radial graph showing the direction of platform rejuvenation on microblade cores.

force directed at the blade face to correct the platform. Undulations on the negative flake scars forming the core platform of specimens indicate the direction of force, and in most cases it tends to be generally parallel to the axis of the core (Figure 21). Platform rejuvenation flakes are sometimes called "core tablets" or "core rejuvenation tablets" (Ackerman 1980:193; Sanger 1970:108), and a total of 20 (containing remnants of the blade face) have been identified in the Campus Site collections (Figure 22). These are spalls with distinctive multifaceted platforms formed by the proximal negative scars left by former microblade removals. Since the rejuvenation removes a portion of one or both sides of the core, the lateral margins of the spall often end abruptly in a flat facet perpendicular to the plane of the flake's dorsal surface (the former core platform). This creates a markedly triangular or rectangular cross section. One of the lateral margins of the spall will have served as the platform for flakes that shaped the core platform, and thus the spall will have a series of unidirectional negative scars on its dorsal surface. The rejuvenation flakes tend to be longer than they are wide. In some cases the scars of former microblade removals on the platform of the core tablet do not show the negative bulbs

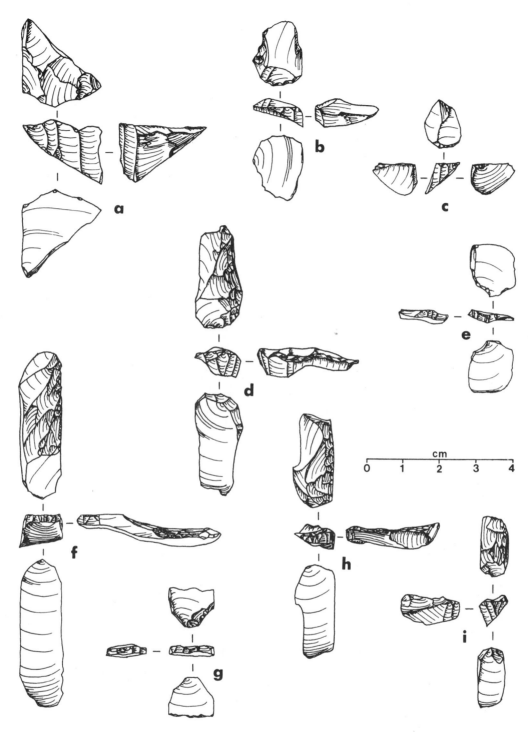

Figure 22. Microblade core rejuvenation flakes with blade face remnant; a. (#3-182), b. (#3-180), c. (66-2578), d. (3-179), e. (#66-554), f. (3-174), g. (66-2657), h. (3-357), i. (66-1043).

of force, indicating removal of two core tablets in succession without any microblade production in between. Quite often the core tablets display a dorsal surface reflecting an earlier core tablet removal. In many cases the spalls end in a hinge fracture.

One of the key attributes in identifying rejuvenation flakes is the remnant of the former blade face, with its

series of parallel blade facets definitely associating it with microblade technology. However, there are in the Campus site collection other spalls that have every distinguishing feature of a rejuvenation flake—except for the identifiable remnant of the core's blade face. These spalls: (1) are longer than they are wide, (2) have distinctive triangular or rectangular cross sections caused by the abrupt lateral edge facets of the core, and (3) show a series of unidirectional flake scars on the dorsal surface, emanating from one of the abrupt edges of the spall. The platform of the spall, where force was applied, is either crushed, or more often consists of a single (small) flat facet that was likely a negative microblade scar from a microblade core. These are probably platform rejuvenation flakes, and are counted and treated as such in a separate class. Eight are present in the collection.

Force directed at the blade face is the most common method of platform rejuvenation in the Campus Site microblade technology, and Mauger (1971:19–20) considers it the only one used. However, in some instances force was directed from the side, at a 90-degree angle to the core axis (Figure 21), and in at least one case (judging from a platform rejuvenation flake) it was directed from the back of the core. Two core specimens (Figures 11, b; 17, b) have negative scars on their platforms indicating rejuvenation using force from the side. In the case of CS3-17 the negative scar is very small with a deep bulbar concavity, while in the case of CS67-3125 almost the entire platform element of the core was removed in one broad shallow scar. In neither case is there evidence of successive bulb alignments to accentuate the concavity, as in the platform preparation technique noted earlier that produces the distinctive "gull-wing" flakes.

Only one platform rejuvenation flake (CS3-180) in the Campus Site collection shows evidence of force directed at a 90-degree angle to the core axis, parallel to the axis of the blade face (Figure 22, b). The dorsal surface shows several overlapping step fractures at the proximal end which created a slight concavity, under which the bulb on the ventral surface of the core tablet is somewhat (but not directly) aligned. The removal truncated the blade face, and the proximal ends of the negative blade scars are evident.

The most anomalous platform rejuvenation noted in the Campus Site microblade technology is reflected by Specimen CS3-182, a rejuvenation flake which was removed using force directed from the back of the core (Figure 22, a). Only the distal portion of the flake was recovered, but undulations on the ventral surface clearly show the origin of force. The dorsal surface indicates that previous platform rejuvenation involved force directed at the blade face from various angles of less than 90 degrees to the core axis. The negative scars reflecting microblade removals on the blade face were truncated by the core tablet removal, but in a plane approximately 30 degrees from that of the original core platform. This may not have been considered a successful rejuvenation. The artifact shows small flake scars on the microblade facets where they intersect the ventral surface of the core tablet, very suggestive of use damage as a result of a scraping motion. The angle of about 75 degrees formed by the intersection would be suitable for scraping activity, and would be in line with Cook's (1968) hypothesis regarding microblade core use, but extreme caution is warranted in inferring use wear for an artifact that has been extensively handled over a 50-year period, and in fact in two places the *ventral* surface of the rejuvenation flake shows a small flake scar where it is intersected by the arrises of blade facets.

The process and tools involved in microblade core rejuvenation are not completely clear from inspection of the Campus Site specimens. Mauger (1971:19) states that "the bulbar morphology of the cores and core tablets in the Campus Site collection suggest that rejuvenation was accomplished through soft hammer or indirect percussion, perhaps while the core was still in the vise." The ability to distinguish hard hammer percussion from indirect percussion has been demonstrated using a replicative approach (Crabtree 1967a:60–62), although caution is urged (Callahan 1979:166). While there are certainly microblade cores and platform rejuvenation flakes with subtle undulations and shallow bulbar morphology, there are also indications of hard hammer percussion used for platform rejuvenation in the Campus Site microblade technology. Evidence for hard hammer percussion is lacking on the cores themselves, because in most cases the proximal element of the negative flake scar left by core tablet removal has been taken off by subsequent microblade removals and/or crushing and flaking of the platform surface to correct its angle or otherwise improve its suitability. Mauger (1971:20) notes such crushing as a deliberate step in platform preparation of Campus Site microblade cores, and it is acknowledged by Ackerman (1980:192) as a systematic aspect of microblade technology in the North Pacific coast region. The platform rejuvenation flakes display the best evidence for hard hammer percussion, because in some cases pronounced bulbs and conspicuous undulations strongly suggest use of direct hard hammer percussion (Figure 22, d). Several specimens suggest that hard hammer direct percussion was used to rejuvenate platforms on Campus Site cores, in addition to perhaps soft hammer or indirect percussion methods.

MICROBLADE CORE DISCARD

At some point after a succession of microblade removals and platform rejuvenations, the microblade core became too small or otherwise unsuitable for microblade production—it was "exhausted." Most complete microblades in the Campus Site collection are longer than the microblade facets on the majority of microblade cores, suggesting that the cores were discarded because they could no longer produce microblades of a useful length. Although some microblade cores in the collection have blade faces of lengths comparable to the lengths of microblades in the sample, Mauger (1971:21) suggests that they were discarded because the aboriginal craftsman visualized the effective length of the core's blade face following needed platform rejuvenation, and consequently rejected the core, knowing that rejuvenation would result in too short a blade face.

West (1967:368) and Mauger (1971:22) both point out that—rather than the length of the blade face—the length of the platform element of the microblade core may sometimes be the critical factor in core discard. Specimen CS3-12 (Figure 15, b) is perhaps an example of a such a core, in that average-size microblades could have been produced from the core but the overall length of the core may have made it difficult to keep it positioned in the vise and still remove microblades.

Finally, manufacturing errors may have prompted discard of the microblade core. Poorly oriented rejuvenation attempts produce platform angles or morphology making blade removal impossible and platform correction difficult. Microblade removals ending in step or hinge fractures, rather than feathering out at the base of the core, may have prompted discard in some cases because of the difficulty in correcting the blade face for better microblade production. Few of the cores in the Campus Site collection show such poor blade termination, however.

While the technological processes involved in microblade manufacture may prove to be more useful for comparative purposes, descriptive characteristics of microblade cores are firmly entrenched in the professional literature. Favored attributes include metric features such as the height and chord length of the blade face, and overall specimen length and width (Table 8; see glossary for definitions).

SUMMARY OF THE MICROBLADE TECHNOLOGY

It is useful to summarize the microblade technology of the Campus Site in terms of both the manufacturing process and the artifacts produced. Chert was the only material used; obsidian was not chosen for microblade production (the only evidence to the contrary being a single obsidian microblade). The chert was naturally available as cobbles; rarely, the cobble was split, and microblade production proceeded on the split cobble. More commonly a flake, or less commonly a biface, was selected as the parent piece from which microblades were removed. Preparation of the blade face involved the removal of an initial spall, which was aligned through unifacial and bifacial retouch. Preparation of the platform element was sometimes achieved by a single blow removing the entire top of the piece; more often it was done through steep unifacial or bifacial retouch. The order of initial platform and blade face preparation to one another is uncertain. Microblades were

Table 8. Descriptive statistics for microblade cores (N = 42). Weight is in grams; other measurements are in mm.

	Mean	Minimum	Maximum	S.D.
Core Length	24.1	15.0	45.6	6.4
Core Height	21.6	14.0	29.0	3.7
Core Width	9.5	4.3	17.3	2.5
Core Weight	5.7	0.8	16.0	3.4
Chord Length	9.4	4.0	18.6	3.3
Face Height	20.7	12.0	28.1	3.9

removed from the core unidirectionally, with no core rotation. Rejuvenation of the microblade core platform was most often achieved by a single force applied directly head-on at the blade face, but sometimes it was done by a single force directed from other angles. Still another distinctive method of platform rejuvenation involved the removal of flakes using force directed 90 degrees to the long axis of the core, in which care was taken that each flake removed had its bulb of force directly aligned below the previous removal, thus enhancing the concavity of the scar and providing a more secure purchase for the tool used to remove microblades from the face of the core. Cores were eventually discarded, presumably because they were too small to produce microblades of the desired length, the platform element became too restricted in area, or because of irreconcilable rejuvenation errors or microblade removal errors.

The artifacts produced by microblade technology are distinctive and reflect the manufacturing process. Most microblade cores from the Campus Site are small and wedge-shaped, with a bifacial "keel" or edge opposite the core's platform; the notable exception is the cobble specimen, which is globular-shaped and has a cortex surface opposite the platform. Each core has only one blade face and only one platform. The blade face may retain the remnants of from two to 12 microblade removal scars. Initial microblades are distinguishable by their triangular cross section and unifacially or bifacially worked dorsal surface. A larger but similar spall, termed a trifaced ridge flake, reflects initial platform preparation.

Microblades removed sometimes had two dorsal facets (and were thus triangular in cross section), but more often had three or more dorsal facets. The microblades are relatively small, with a narrow range of metric variability.

Reflecting a force directed at the side of the microblade core, gull-wing flakes are platform rejuvenation flakes with aligned bulbs on their dorsal surface (displaying a negative bulb) and ventral surface (displaying a positive bulb). Platform rejuvenation effected by force directed head-on at the blade face produces long narrow spalls that retain a portion of one or both sides of the core, and have as their platform a remnant of the core blade face showing portions of the scars left by microblade removal. Other, similar core rejuvenation flakes are produced in the same way, differing only in that the flake's platform shows no unambiguously identifiable remnant of the core blade face.

The microblade technology has been one of the most-discussed aspects of the Campus Site, and there are several published summaries of the process and the artifacts produced. The extent to which this restudy's enlarged sample size changes prior characterizations of the collection is discussed at the end of this volume.

Biface Technology

Two distinct artifact forms in the Campus Site collection are indicative of biface technology: bifaces, and biface thinning flakes. Bifaces are flaked across two roughly parallel surfaces, using a common edge as the point from which most flakes are removed. Consequently both faces of the specimen show proximal or near-proximal portions of negative flake scars originating from the same edge. Some specimens in the Campus Site collection were worked on both surfaces but from different edges for one surface than the other, likely reflecting initial entry of a flake into the biface reduction system, and were also classified as bifaces in this analysis (although in such cases no portion of the specimen's edge displays intersecting proximal negative flake scars). With questionable specimens, the relative length of the flake scars across the piece was a factor in distinguishing bifaces from retouched pieces, with the former tending to display lesser edge angles and longer scars extending across the surface. Biface thinning flakes are diagnostic artifacts resulting from biface manufacture, discriminated on the basis of: (a) a multifaceted flake platform, (b) an acute platform-to-dorsal surface angle, (c) and a pronounced lip on the ventral surface just above the bulb of percussion (Morlan 1973:17; Mobley 1982:91). Other shapes and sizes of flakes are produced by biface reduction, but are not easily distinguishable from those produced by other technologies, such as core/flake reduction (Newcomer 1971, Kalin 1981, Stahle and Dunn 1982).

The biface manufacturing process first involves selection of raw material. Of the five different raw materials identified in this analysis, only quartz is not represented in the biface assemblage. The majority (92%) of the bifaces are made of chert, but also present are a few specimens made of obsidian and the two kinds of coarse stone. The coarse material with conchoidal fracture (N = 1) and the coarse material with tabular fracture (N = 4) were used strictly for a group designated as "battered bifaces." Each of the three obsidian bifaces is in a different category: irregular, lanceolate point, and notched point.

Thermal alteration is evident on four (4.4%) specimens in the biface assemblage: two distal tips, one round basal fragment, and one irregular biface.

Options for reducing a stone into a biface depend on the size and form of the stone and the preferences of the craftsman. Beginning with the stone slab or cobble, he can immediately begin bifacial flaking and reduce the cobble into a biface, discarding the resulting flakes, or he can apply a core/flake strategy to first remove large flakes from the cobble, and then work the flakes into bifaces (the cobble core being either retained for further manipulation or discarded). Only one biface contains a cortex surface suggesting that a cobble (or cortical flake) was selected as the parent rock. A few bifaces exhibit remnants of a large flake scar surface which would suggest origin as a flake, but rarely is there a positive bulb of percussion which would definitely document a flake origin. Nonetheless, despite the dearth of flake cores, many of the bifaces probably originated as flakes. Possible exceptions are three bifaces made of coarse silicified shales and mudstones which display tabular fracture; small slabs of this material may have been modified directly into bifaces.

Most of the bifacial artifacts in the Campus Site collection are in latter stages of reduction. Not a single specimen could be characterized as a "rough-out," referring to very chunky bifaces that retain considerable cortex (Mobley 1982:91). Some specimens exhibit blocky to biconvex cross sections and rather sinuous edges (and some do display remnants of cortex), but the majority appear to be preforms or finished tools (or fragments thereof), with a relatively thin lenticular cross section and even margins. It is useful to divide the biface assemblage into gross categories: (1) irregularly shaped bifaces, which consist of broken and unfinished specimens, (2) battered specimens, and (3) unbattered, symmetrically shaped (broken and unbroken) specimens. The latter category can be further subdivided into: (a) oval bifaces, (b) triangular bifaces, (c) relatively complete lanceolate points, (d) round basal fragments, (e) square basal fragments, (f) distal fragments, or tips, and (g) notched points. Descriptive statistics for continuous variables monitored in the biface assemblage are presented in Table 9.

IRREGULARLY SHAPED BIFACES

Many bifaces in the Campus site collections are irregularly shaped pieces of stone with varying degrees of bifacial flaking. They tend to be thick in cross section, and most of the edges are formed by intersecting flake scars. Their edges are more sinuous than specimens in other biface categories. They appear to represent an intermediate stage in biface reduction, and are in that sense unfinished. Some have edges with one or more flat facets per-

Table 9. Descriptive statistics for continuous variables monitored in the biface assemblage. Weights are in grams; other measurements are maximum dimensions in cm.

BIFACE CLASS	Length	Width	Thickness	Weight
Irregular	11.6 mean	7.5 mean	7.1 mean	7.0 mean
(N = 40)	1.0 min	0.6 min	1.1 min	0.2 min
	41.7 max	26.8 max	19.3 max	36.4 max
	11.4 SD	8.0 SD	4.5 SD	9.2 SD
Battered	19.6 mean	8.9 mean	14.2 mean	58.3 mean
(N = 8)	5.4 min	3.5 min	8.5 min	21.5 min
	99.9 max	41.5 max	21.7 max	145.8 max
	32.5 SD	13.2 SD	4.2 SD	42.3 SD
Oval to Elongate	14.0 mean	9.5 mean	11.5 mean	18.9 mean
(N = 5)	5.5 min	1.9 min	8.3 min	7.9 min
	46.3 max	36.2 max	17.4 max	27.0 max
	18.1 SD	14.9 SD	3.6 SD	7.6 SD
Triangular	11.3 mean	7.5 mean	5.4 mean	7.0 mean
(N = 4)	3.3 min	2.6 min	3.9 min	2.4 min
	33.6 max	21.6 max	7.3 max	11.9 max
	14.9 SD	9.4 SD	1.5 SD	4.1 SD
Lanceolate	12.7 mean	5.4 mean	8.5 mean	9.6 mean
Point	3.0 min	1.7 min	6.9 min	4.3 min
(N = 7)	58.4 max	24.5 max	10.0 max	15.7 max
	20.2 SD	8.5 SD	1.2 SD	4.3 SD
Round Basal	3.0 mean	2.2 mean	7.6 mean	5.8 mean
Fragment	1.6 min	1.4 min	4.7 min	0.8 min
(N = 9)	5.1 max	3.1 max	10.5 max	15.7 max
	1.3 SD	0.5 SD	2.2 SD	5.1 SD
Square Basal	2.0 mean	1.8 mean	5.0 mean	1.7 mean
Fragment	1.7 min	1.1 min	3.5 min	0.8 min
(N = 5)	2.9 max	2.2 max	6.2 max	3.4 max
	0.5 SD	0.5 SD	1.2 SD	1.0 SD
Tips	8.2 mean	5.6 mean	5.7 mean	4.7 mean
(N = 16)	0.5 min	0.6 min	1.6 min	0.1 min
	39.6 max	20.2 max	9.2 max	13.0 max
	9.7 SD	6.0 SD	2.4 SD	4.3 SD
Notched Point	38.5 mean	22.5 mean	7.9 mean	6.3 mean
(N = 2)	36.9 min	21.6 min	6.6 min	6.3 min
	40.0 max	23.3 max	9.1 max	6.4 max
	2.2 SD	1.2 SD	1.8 SD	0.1 SD

pendicular to the plane of the specimen. Flake scars with platforms originating at those facets indicate that the piece was still in the process of reduction, rather than the facet being simply the result of a post-manufacture snap or other biface fracture. All are of chert except for a single obsidian specimen, and none are thermally altered.

Specimens with one or more unaltered facets forming part of their edge (perpendicular to the plane of the biface), with no flake scars emanating from them, are considered broken rather than unfinished. Breakage probably occurred during tool use on some specimens, during man-

ufacture on others. All are of chert. Severe potlidding attests to thermal alteration of one specimen. Of all the irregularly shaped bifaces, 27 (68%) are fragments, and the remainder are considered to be unfinished.

BATTERED BIFACES

Symmetrical battered bifaces are distinct from other bifaces not only by virtue of edge damage but also size; battered bifaces tend to be relatively large. Step fractures during manufacture were encouraged by the character of the raw material for the few silicified shale and mudstone pieces with tabular fracture. But other battered specimens are made of chert or coarse materials supporting conchoidal fracture. If the step fractures are due to use, which for some specimens seems reasonable given their severity, then these bifaces are finished tools. In two instances only one edge is severely battered, leaving the other much sharper, suggesting that one edge was deliberately blunted or "backed" to facilitate hand-held use. Most of the specimens are somewhat asymmetrical (Figure 23, b; 24, a). An exception is one of the largest specimens in this category, which tends toward a pear-shaped outline (Figure 23, c). A second exception is a large, but more elongate, specimen with a distinct point (Figure 23, h).

OVAL TO ELONGATE BIFACES

Four specimens are flaked into oval to elongate biface forms. Some fragments are characterized as oval in shape by assuming symmetry and estimating the missing portion. The degree of elongation and symmetry varies within this category (Figure 24, b, c), but the outlines of the specimens in between the extremes show a gradual gradation that does not support division into morphological subsets. Such artifacts are sometimes assigned the functional term "knife" in other typologies (Aigner 1986:128; Holmes 1986:47–50).

TRIANGULAR BIFACES

One complete biface in the collection is triangular in outline, and three trapezoidal biface fragments (with the shorter parallel side formed by a break) were once triangular when complete (Figure 25, a–d). Edges are gently convex or straight, as are the bases. All are of chert, and none are thermally altered. One specimen (Figure 25, b) is unusual for the expansive cortical surface on one side. Another specimen (Figure 25, a) is notable for polished arrises on one surface and evidence of basal grinding.

LANCEOLATE POINTS

This category contains artifacts that have been described as projectile points in earlier reports (Nelson 1937, Rainey 1939). The seven relatively complete lanceolate (contracting stemmed) points in the Campus Site collections show some variability, and are important for understand-

ing the more numerous point fragments. Basal grinding is apparent on all seven specimens (indicated in Figure 26 by dots around the edge of the specimens). Three specimens have extensive grinding on the base and extending up the blade margins to over a third of the total length. With one exception (Figure 26, e) the bases have rounded or gently rectangular outlines. In two instances (Figure 26, c, e) the base consists of a flat facet where flake scar platforms do not intersect. Whether the basal facet began as a snap or a burin blow is not clear, since in all cases flaking has partially reduced the facet from its original size. However, one specimen does have a possible burin blow emanating *from* the base and extending a short ways down the lateral edge (Figure 26, a).

These lanceolate bifaces are a recognized component of the Campus Site collections. Three were figured and discussed by Rainey (1939:384–386). He suggested that the artifacts were "spearpoints" or "arrowheads," but concluded that "in the absence of lateral notches or stems there is no indication of hafting." On the contrary, hafting is suggested by the basal and basal-lateral grinding. With these complete specimens in mind, biface fragments (described below) may be more accurately characterized as basal fragments by virtue of grinding. None of the complete lanceolate points exhibit grinding or wear on their distal (more pointed) ends, a fact that also aids in identifying fragments. In further support of these lanceolate points as characteristic of the Campus Site assemblage is the catalog entry for the collection sent to the Soviet Union in the 1930s, which mentions two "leaf-shaped points" among the artifacts.

ROUND BASAL FRAGMENTS

Triangular bifaces with one side formed by an unmodified facet or "break" are usually classified as "point/knife tip" in the catalogs of the various Campus Site collections, referring to the distal elements of bifacial tools. Many of these fragments display gently rounded bifacial ends, and about half of them have very dull edges. Comparison with complete specimens in the collection is instructive, because those have heavily edge-ground bases and several—sometimes described as "leaf-shaped points"—are rather bi-pointed with rounded bases. Most basal fragments of such points would be indistinguishable from distal elements except for the edge-grinding. Thus the pointed biface fragments are divided into those with edge-grinding and those without. Those without edge-grinding

Figure 23. Large artifacts; a. tabular piece (#3-201), b., c., h. battered bifaces (#67-1230, #3-203, #3-194), d. cobble spall (#3-202), e. ground stone (#3-191), f–g. hammerstones (#3-186, #3-204), i. flake core (#3-409), j. ground stone abrader (#3-185).

a

b

c

d

e

f

g

h

i

j

CS-3-202

cs-3-186

0 1 2 3 4 5
cm

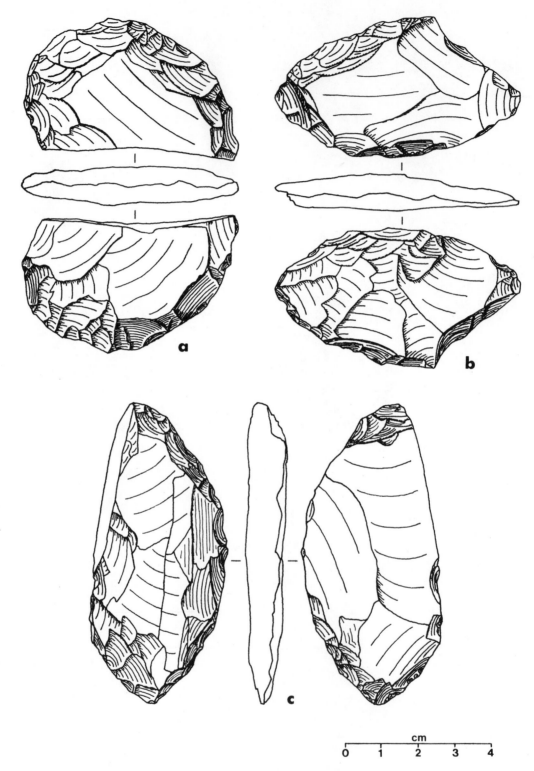

cm
0 1 2 3 4

Figure 24. Bifaces; a. battered biface (#3-340), b–c. oval bifaces (#3-40, #66-207).

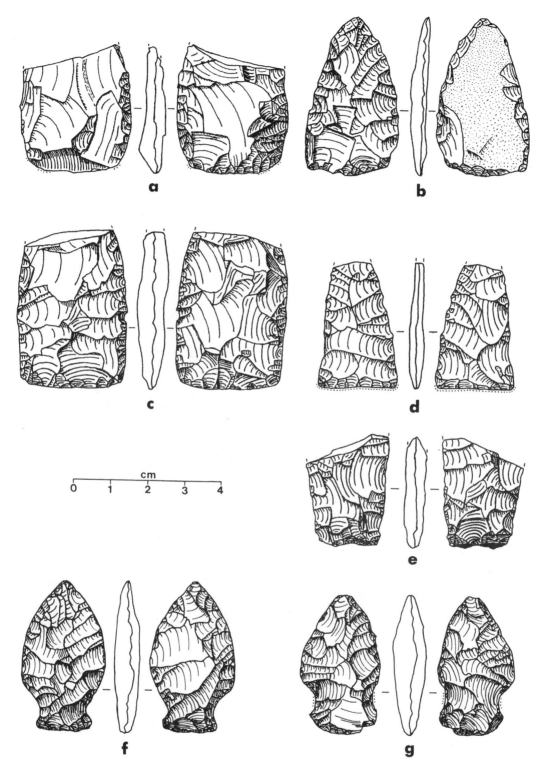

Figure 25. Bifaces; a–d. triangular (#3-341, #3-58, #71-4804, #67-1346), e. square basal fragment (#3-55), f–g. notched points (#66-690, #3-36).

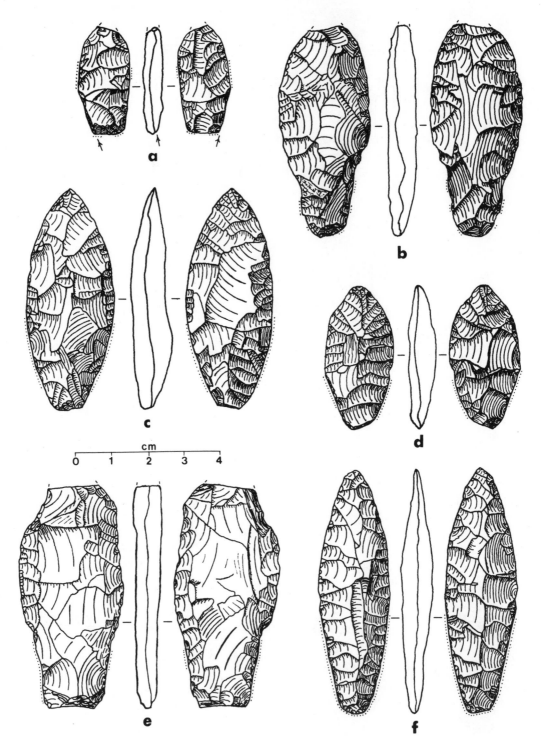

Figure 26. Bifaces; a. lanceolate, burinized (#3-56), b–f. lanceolate (#3-57, #67-229, #3-41, #A-12636, #3-54).

are likely the distal elements of bifacial tools, and those with edge-grinding are likely the proximal elements of edge-ground points like the complete ones in the collection.

Identification of the edge-ground biface fragments as the proximal elements of basally ground points is further reinforced by the degree of "pointedness," for with only one exception the edge-ground specimens have a more rounded point than the sharp-edged specimens (Figure 27, b, d, f, g). Nine specimens, all of chert, are classed as basally ground (proximal) elements of bifacial tools (likely lanceolate points).

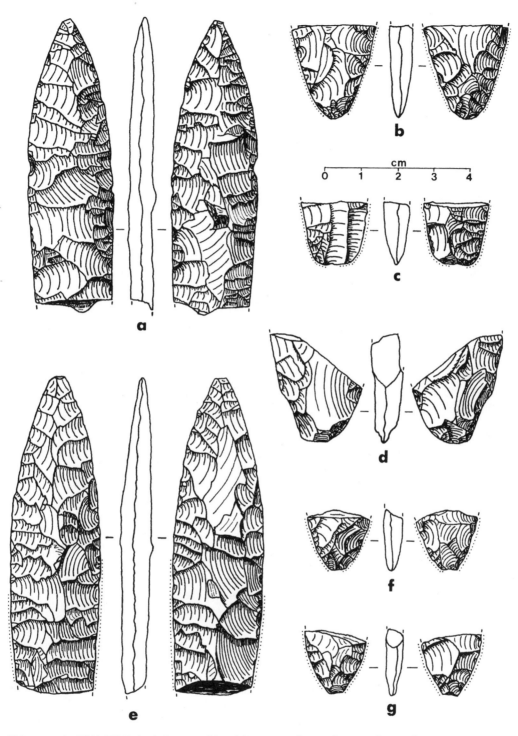

Figure 27. Bifaces; a. tip (#66-2700), b, d, f–g. round basal fragments (#3-47, #3-198, #3-50, #3-51), c. square basal fragment (#66-1289), e. tip, not from Campus Site proper, but found on the UAF campus (#9348).

BIFACE TIPS

The remainder of the triangular biface fragments consist of 16 specimens considered to be distal elements of bifacial tools. They range from very small fragments to a long specimen which is probably missing only a small fraction of its base (Figure 27, a). One specimen has a long narrow blade outline and rather diamond-like cross-section, but there is no wear to suggest use as a drill. All are of chert, and one is thermally altered.

SQUARE BASAL FRAGMENTS

For want of a better term, "square basal fragments" refer to trapezoidal biface fragments for which the long parallel edge consists of a break, and they probably represent the proximal elements of bifacial points. The complete lanceolate points all show either gently rounded or "squared-off" proximal elements, and all show various degrees of basal grinding. One specimen (Figure 27, c) has a prominent basal thinning scar approaching a fluted point appearance, but—although fluted points with possible PaleoIndian connotations are known in the Arctic and subarctic (Clark 1984b)—the morphology of the Campus Site specimen does not make it a convincing fluted point. Of five square basal fragments, two show some edge-grinding (Figure 27, c). Another (Figure 25, e) has a (slightly retouched) flat facet forming the edge or base, which is also a feature of two complete lanceolate points.

NOTCHED POINTS

The last bifaces to be discussed are two notched points. An obsidian specimen (Figure 25, g) was recovered in the 1930s, and a chert example was recovered in 1966 (Figure 25, f). Both specimens are broad-bladed bifaces with shallow side-notches.

BIFACE THINNING FLAKES

Biface thinning flakes provide additional information about the biface technology at the Campus Site. A total of 468 specimens were recovered, of which 94.7% were of chert, 2.4% were of obsidian, 2.6% were of the coarse material with conchoidal fracture, and a single specimen was of quartz. These raw material frequencies are comparable to those for regular flakes. Only 16 of the bifacial thinning flakes are thermally altered. Roughly a third (38.6%) of the biface thinning flakes are complete, the remainder being proximal fragments. Most (65.2%) of the specimens weigh 0.1 grams or less.

SUMMARY OF THE BIFACE TECHNOLOGY

The biface technology practiced at the Campus Site can be characterized in terms of the reduction process and the resulting artifacts. The reduction process began with raw material selection: chert was most commonly used, but so was obsidian and coarse stone with either conchoidal or tabular fracture. Apparently most raw materials were initially processed at the geologic source, while obsidian was often brought to the site in cobble form; this matter is discussed more fully in the Site Activities chapter. Biface thinning flakes of the same raw materials represented by the bifaces document that the final stages of biface manufacture took place at the Campus Site.

Because most of the evidence of biface technology in the Campus Site collection reflects the later stages of reduction, the process is less thoroughly discussed in favor of discussing the more static matter of the resulting artifacts. Broken and unfinished bifaces are the most common form, for which the intended shape can only be guessed. A set of large bifaces show battered edges, indicating severe use as a tool. Several triangular bifaces are present, as are bifaces ranging from an oval to elongate shape. A distinctive point type, represented by several relatively complete specimens, can be characterized as a lanceolate or gently contracting stemmed form. Grinding on the lateral and basal elements of these complete points is an aid in identifying additional biface fragments as the basal element of similar specimens; these basal fragments (and the complete specimens) can be further differentiated into those with rather rounded bases, and those that are more straight-based. The collection also contains pointed biface fragments, or tips, of unknown function. Completing the biface collection are two side-notched points.

Macroblade Technology

Although the term "blade" was used in describing artifacts recovered at the Campus Site in the 1930s, it was used indiscriminately to mean long narrow bifaces and unifaces (Rainey 1939:384–387). A macroblade industry, in a technological sense, was not recognized at the Campus Site until the excavations of the 1960s (Hosley and Mauger 1967:8–9). It is not a dominant component of the assemblage, yet future research may determine it to be temporally, culturally, or functionally significant in understanding the prehistory of central Alaska. No macroblade cores were recovered, and the macroblade assemblage is limited to twelve specimens (including six showing retouch) with parallel or only slightly subparallel edges, and long narrow parallel negative scars on the dorsal surface creating a prismatic cross section. Assignment of artifacts to the blade category was conservative, and several candidates with relatively prismatic cross sections and high length-to-width ratios were excluded because they lacked parallel edges or sufficiently parallel dorsal scars. Length is often a factor in classifying macroblades as well, since they tend to be much longer than they are wide, but because the Campus Site specimens are all fragments that criterion does not readily apply. The attributes of width and thickness do readily discriminate microblades and macroblades into two populations, however. The Campus Site has produced no blade cores and few flake cores or core fragments, and most of the latter are too small to produce macroblades.

All the macroblade specimens are made of chert, but macroscopic inspection suggests that three are of the same specific material, a grey chert that weathers to a light tan (the same stone as many of the microblades and microblade cores). These three specimens are also of similar thickness and width, although all are fragments and all have been retouched. Of two proximal fragments, only one actually retains a significant portion of the platform. The platform is small and multifaceted, with a very abraded and rounded intersection between the platform and the dorsal surface, indicating conscientious platform preparation. Any indication of blade face preparation such as realignment of dorsal ridges (to help direct the detachment of the blade from the core) has been obliterated by subsequent retouching. The macroblades exhibit a maximum of five dorsal blade removal facets.

The remaining macroblades are of different colored and textured cherts, and do not give the impression that they were produced methodically by a knapper specializing in macroblade production. They may be incidental products of core/flake technology. The total macroblade assemblage of twelve specimens contains only three complete specimens. Another three are proximal fragments, however, providing six specimens with which to evaluate platform preparation. The platforms are multifaceted, with tiny hinge and step fractures on the platform at its junction with the dorsal surface, and—to a lesser extent—on the dorsal surface at its junction with the platform. Two specimens are thermally altered. Triangular cross sections are in a minority, with most specimens showing three or more dorsal facets, but this observation is reduced in meaning by the fact that half the assemblage consists of fragments. A single complete specimen varies from trapezoidal to triangular in cross section, proceeding from the proximal to the distal end, illustrating the fallacy in basing cross section descriptions on fragments.

Subsequent modification of macroblades took three forms, one of which—retouching (performed on six specimens)—is discussed later in this chapter. Another operation is reflected by a medial macroblade fragment which was broken by deliberate snapping. The cross section of the blade appears to have been symmetrically trapezoidal, with a dorsal facet parallel to the ventral surface. Two prominent partial cones are apparent adjacent to that dorsal facet, indicating where force was applied to truncate the proximal and distal ends of the specimen (Figure 28, e). A small flake originating from that same dorsal facet removed part of one lateral edge, apparently in an attempt to eliminate a coarse inclusion.

Snapping of prismatic macroblades in this manner is characteristic of British gunflint manufacture as practiced by craftsmen of Brandon, according to discussion and illustrations by Whitthoft (1966:19, 36), Woodward (1960:30–33), and Smith (1960:46–47), and it is worth discussing the technology as it has a bearing on the possibility of historic aboriginal activity at the Campus Site. The Campus Site specimen is not of the dark flint quarried commercially in England, nor is it of the "blond" translucent flint commonly quarried in France. Instead it is of a chalky whitish grey material with a coarse dark grainy inclusion. The material is not strikingly out of place among the other rock types represented in the Campus Site collection, although no specimens of identical material were noted. It would appear illogical that a flawed European gunflint (containing a coarse inclusion) would be exported, but correspondence between European producers and North American consumers does contain complaints that substandard gunflints were exported. Commercial gunflints (possibly from Galicia in Russian Poland) recovered from the Russian post of St. Michael on Norton Sound are manufactured very differently from the English method, but the material may be similar to the Campus Site specimen, described as "a porous, mat-surfaced, non-glossy chalk flint, light grey to grey-black in color, with many tiny spherical whitish blotches and dots" (Witthoft 1966:39).

Although the snapped macroblade is technologically comparable to English gunflints, snapped macroblades are not unknown in prehistoric Alaskan lithic technology. Macroblade assemblages from the Aleutians contain similar artifacts—prismatic medial fragments with definite bulbs indicating deliberate truncation (Aigner 1970:67). However, the latter do not show such pronounced cones as do gunflints produced with the Brandon method, possibly because the Aleutian specimens were snapped using force applied directly to the dorsal surface with the wider ventral surface fully supported, compared to the Brandon method in which the dorsal surface of the macroblade is supported on an anvil or "stake" and force applied to the ventral surface. It is the stake that produces the pronounced cone (Woodward 1960:31). Digressing further from strictly technological matters in search of explanations for the artifact's presence at the Campus Site, it should be stated that several alumni of the 1930s remember no formal or informal campus group involved with muzzle-loading firearms.

In the Campus Site collection there is little difficulty in discriminating between microblades and macroblades. A bivariate plot of thickness and width (the two variables most useful for characterizing fragments) for the combined microblade and macroblade assemblage shows no overlap between the two artifact classes (Figure 29). Descriptive statistics for continuous variables monitored in the macroblade assemblage are presented in Table 10.

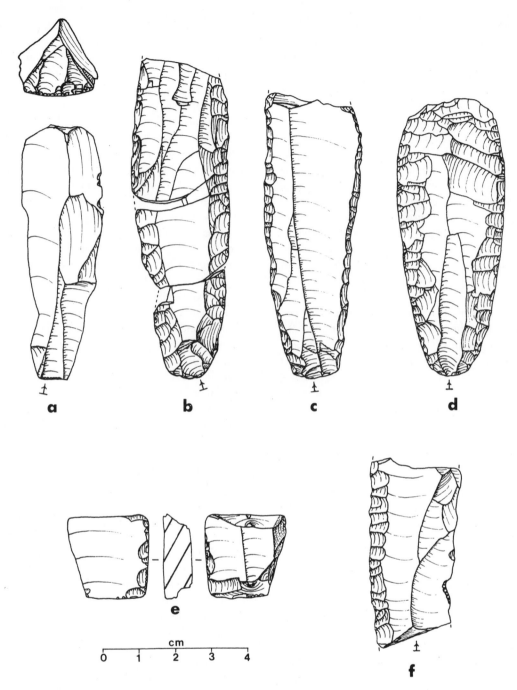

Figure 28. Macroblades. a. distally retouched (#67-1750), b, c, f, laterally retouched (#3-157, #3-160, #3-163), d. laterally retouched with flute scar (#3-99), e. snapped medial fragment (#3-114).

SUMMARY OF THE MACROBLADE TECHNOLOGY

The macroblade specimens are easily separable from the microblade specimens based on their larger size, but the former are not a dominant element in the Campus Site collection. No macroblade cores were recovered, reducing information available about the production process and raising doubts as to whether the macroblades were pro-

duced at the site. The specimens are made of chert, and have three or more dorsal facets.

Detailed comparisons between the Campus Site macroblades and assemblages from other sites may be limited, since the small sample size allows little estimate of the actual range of variability that may have existed in the macroblade technological system. It is a method of stone manipulation distinct from other technologies present at

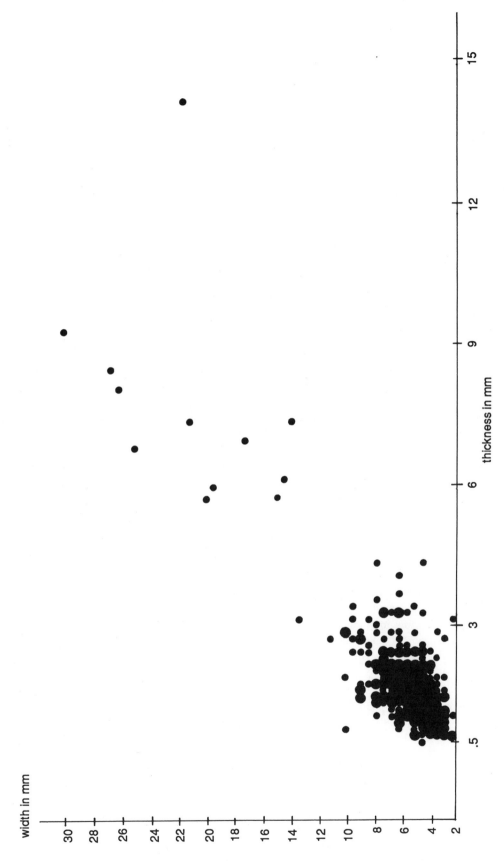

Figure 29. Bivariate plot of macroblade and microblade width and thickness. The large dots indicate more than one artifact with the same measurements.

53

Table 10. Descriptive statistics for continuous variables monitored in the macroblade assemblage. Weight is in grams, other measurements in mm.

ARTIFACT CLASS	Length	Width	Thickness	Weight
MACROBLADES	51.7 mean	20.9 mean	7.4 mean	8.3 mean
	29.9 min	13.4 min	3.1 min	1.6 min
	72.8 max	30.2 max	14.3 max	20.5 max
	21.7 SD	5.4 SD	2.7 SD	8.4 SD
	4 = N	12 = N	12 = N	4 = N

the site, however, and it is of note that a macroblade industry should be found in the same site with core/flake, biface, and microblade industries.

Core/Flake Technology

The artifact classes recognized as products of core/flake technology are cores, flakes, and nondiagnostic shatter. Tasks involved in core/flake technology include selecting raw material, testing it for flaking qualities, and removing flakes. The modified cobble, now termed a core, may then be used as a tool, or the flakes may be eventually used as tools with or without further modification into bifaces, retouched specimens, etc., at which time they enter another lithic technology subsystem.

Flake cores are products of core/flake technology, as are flakes. Other lithic technologies also produce flakes that are not necessarily distinguishable from those produced by core/flake technology, but they are included here under the heading of core/flake technology nonetheless. Thus the flake collection includes specimens produced by core/flake technology, and undoubtedly includes specimens produced incidentally in the manufacture of microblade cores, bifaces, retouched specimens and other chipped stone items. Some flakes are diagnostic of certain knapping methods depending on the lithic technology and the degree of analytical discrimination, such as biface thinning flakes (discussed earlier as a product of biface technology) and lithic debris resulting from microblade core rejuvenation. All such diagnostic flakes are discussed elsewhere under the lithic technology to which they pertain.

NONDIAGNOSTIC SHATTER

Experimentation with prospective cores often results in sudden disintegration of the rock, producing artifacts termed nondiagnostic shatter, or NDS (Binford and Quimby 1963:278–279; Mobley 1982:91). NDS is not common in the Campus Site, with 69 specimens representing 0.7% of the total collection. A disproportionately high percentage of the quartz assemblage is composed of NDS, reflecting the material's intractable flaking qualities (Crabtree 1967b:11) as well as the difficulty in differentiating natural cleavage planes from culturally produced flake scars.

FLAKE CORES

Flake cores are not common in the Campus Site collection, with a total of 17 present. The cores reflect four material types: chert, obsidian, quartz, and the coarse-grained rock with conchoidal fracture. However, many different chert colors and qualities noticeable in the total assemblage are not represented in the core collection. Most of the cores have stream-rounded cortical remnants of the original cobble surface; generally the larger cores have the most cortex. One large core shows severe battering on part of its cortical surface (Figure 23, i). In several cases, a cobble was used directly as a core, whereas in other cases a large thick flake was struck from a cobble, and the flake was then used as a core from which subsequent flakes were struck (Figure 30, b, e). Only one core is thermally altered. There is a considerable range in size for the cores (Table 11). Most of the cores reflect rotation during flake removal. An exception, which has many flake scars emanating unidirectionally from a cortex platform, joins with a rotated core to indicate that both options—unidirectional and multidirectional flaking—were practiced by the same craftsmen at their discretion.

FLAKES

The majority of the Campus Site artifacts are flakes, most of which could be called lithic debris, as they are presumed to have been discarded. Because of the conservative attitude taken in identifying retouched specimens, the lithic debris category includes pieces with subtle edge modification that would probably be termed "utilized" flakes by other researchers. The flakes assumed to be from the 1930s excavations were excluded from this analysis because they are uncataloged, unprovenienced, and may be mixed with material from other sites. This applies to over 1,200 larger flakes residing loose in three cigar boxes, weighing a total of 2,015 grams. Accompanying the boxes are cautionary notes from University of Alaska Museum personnel, stating, for example, that "one flake found in this box was from the Dixthada Site, so there

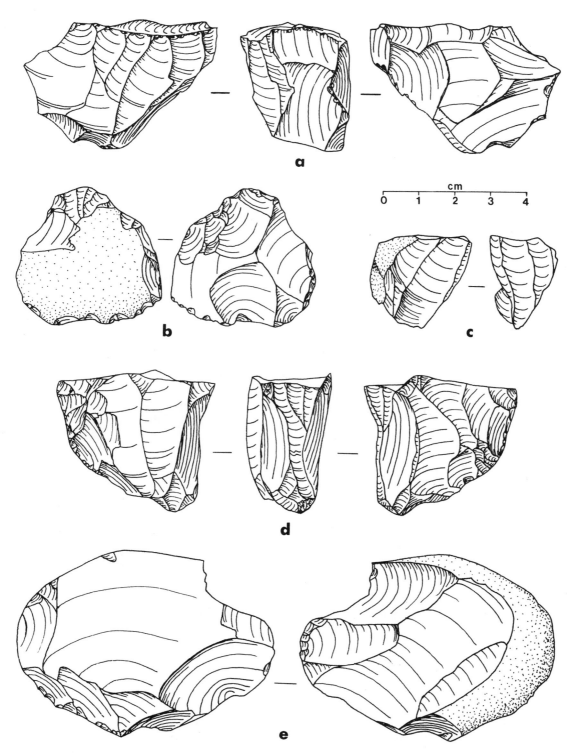

Figure 30. Flake cores. a.–e. (#66-825, #66-2781, #3-448, #3-66, #3-419).

Table 11. Descriptive statistics for weight of cores and flakes, according to raw material, in grams.

Raw Material	Cores	Flakes
Coarse: conchoidal fracture	207.3 mean	1.5 mean
	20.4 min	0.1 min
	370.4 max	39.2 max
	143.3 SD	4.4 SD
	5 = N	204 = N
Coarse: tabular fracture	–	– mean
	–	0.1 min
	–	2.5 max
	–	1.7 SD
	0 = N	2 = N
Chert	30.3 mean	0.3 mean
	8.8 min	0.1 min
	71.5 max	112.9 max
	24.7 SD	2.2 SD
	9 = N	7,021 = N
Obsidian	15.8 mean	0.4 mean
	–	0.1 min
	–	6.2 max
	–	0.7 SD
	1 = N	180 = N
Quartz	366.9 mean	5.0 mean
	12.6 min	0.1 min
	721.1 max	35.2 max
	501.0 SD	11.1 SD
	2 = N	10 = N

could be others mixed in as well." Located in one box of flakes and standing out in light of that comment, for example, is a tall, slender microblade core, unlike the other Campus Site specimens in form or raw material, with several lichen growth marks on its surface. It was excluded from analysis. Meaningful quantitative comparisons between artifact frequencies in the Campus Site assemblage must be based on the 1966 and later collections.

The flakes range in size from very small specimens weighing 0.1 gram or less, up to the largest specimen weighing 112.9 grams. The total weight distribution of flakes for each raw material is skewed heavily toward the left in favor of many very small flakes, because the recovery effort in 1967 used two gauges of screen, sifting first through ¼ inch mesh, then through ⅛ inch mesh. This procedure caught many very small specimens weighing 0.1 gram or less, creating a one-tailed weight distribution curve.

All five raw materials are represented in the flake assemblage (Table 11), although their frequencies differ significantly from the frequency of cores of those materials. The differing availability and workability of each raw material warrants discussion of flake attributes separately for each material.

The coarse material with conchoidal fracture constitutes 2.8% of the flake assemblage. Of the 204 speci-

mens, 63 are complete, 21 are proximal fragments, 41 are medial fragments, and 79 are distal fragments. Platform characteristics on the complete and proximal specimens break down into 67 multifaceted and 17 single-faceted examples. Most of the specimens are flakes with no cortex on their dorsal surface (termed interior flakes), but six have some cortex (termed secondary decortication flakes), and one has over 90% cortex (termed a primary decortication flake). No examples of this material are thermally altered.

The small sample size of two limits generalizations about the coarse material with tabular fracture. The one proximal and one medial fragment are both interior flakes, and the platform of the former specimen is characterized as indeterminate. Neither was thermally altered.

The chert flake collection contains 1,292 complete specimens, 1,157 proximal fragments, 2,714 medial fragments, 1,853 distal fragments, and five of indeterminate character. The complete and proximal specimens contain all platform types identified in the analysis, with 41 cortical platforms, 865 single-faceted platforms, and 1,538 multifaceted platforms. With 6,902 examples, interior flakes comprise the majority of the assemblage, the remainder consisting of 92 secondary flakes, and 26 primary flakes. Thermal alteration is evident on 176 specimens, or 2.5% of the chert assemblage.

Of the 180 obsidian flakes, 57 are complete, 27 are proximal fragments, 32 are medial fragments, and 64 are distal fragments. Four specimens have cortex platforms, 20 have single-faceted platforms, and 57 have multifaceted platforms. Most of the sample consists of interior flakes, with only seven secondary and no primary decortication flakes. No thermal alteration is evident.

The quartz flakes are composed of two complete specimens, five medial fragments, and three distal fragments. One of the complete flakes has a cortex platform, the other has a multifaceted platform. Eight specimens are interior flakes, one is secondary, and one is primary. None are thermally altered.

SUMMARY OF CORE/FLAKE TECHNOLOGY

Cores, flakes, and nondiagnostic shatter (NDS) all attest to a core/flake technology at the Campus Site. Chert, obsidian, quartz, and the coarse-grained material with conchoidal fracture were manipulated in this manner. Some preliminary testing of the raw material must have been done at the material source, since NDS is relatively infrequent, as is cortex on the platforms and dorsal surfaces of flakes. Cores—made from cobbles or flakes—are few in number, show a large range in size, and were usually rotated for flake removal.

The flake lot constitutes the majority of the Campus Site collection, with over 7,000 specimens. Most are very small (weighing less than 0.5 grams), recovered by screening during the 1966, 1967, and 1971 excavations.

Retouched Specimens

Retouching is the process of unifacially removing short, usually overlapping flakes from the edge of a piece of stone—either a flake, macroblade, microblade, or fragments thereof. In this analysis, retouching is considered to have been done deliberately through percussion or pressure knapping techniques, with the intent of creating a retouched tool. A similar (but usually less pronounced) edge may be created incidently by dragging the edge of a specimen against the surface of another object, thereby removing a series of flakes from the specimen's margin. The result of this latter operation is sometimes termed "use-retouch" (Morlan 1973:18). The distinction between deliberate and accidental retouch is ignored in this study primarily because no functional analyses were performed upon the lithic specimens. Also, the curation circumstances likely have caused considerable inadvertent post-excavation edge damage, lessening the possibility of detailed and accurate characterizations of purposeful versus accidental retouch. Kamminga (1979:371) comments that up to 40% of the edges of specimens may be fractured simply through transport and handling within cloth bags.

Specimens were conservatively assigned to the retouched category using macroscopic observation, so that those with nonpatterned, nonoverlapping nicks were excluded (to be considered as unmodified flakes, macroblades, or microblades). The retouched category contains specimens that have been described as "scrapers" in other analyses (Nelson 1935:356, Hosley and Mauger 1967:9), but this functional term is avoided in the present analysis. Implicit functional assumptions about stone tools based solely on morphological characteristics have been consistently denounced, and "one outstanding example is the term 'scraper', which is still employed to describe a wide range of retouched stone artifacts, and which almost certainly has little functional integrity as a category" (Hayden and Kamminga 1979:3).

The selection of raw material for retouching was dependent on the array of raw material chosen for manipulation in any one of the lithic technologies—core/flake reduction, macroblade production, and microblade production. The retouching process was applied to the products of all three technologies, and is best discussed individually for each.

RETOUCHED MACROBLADES

Six of the twelve Campus Site macroblades are retouched. Three are retouched on both lateral blade edges and a fourth specimen is retouched on one edge only. On all four the retouch is confined to the dorsal surface (Figure 28,

b–c, f), enhancing their plano-convex cross section, and the entire length is modified.

One large complete macroblade displays dorsal retouch on the distal end (Figure 28, a). Several flake removals on the distal end create a truncation that is at a right angle to the long axis of the artifact, with an edge angle of 65 degrees. Numerous small hinge and step fractures are present on the retouched facet at the point where it intersects the ventral surface.

The sixth retouched macroblade displays cones of force indicating deliberate snapping, in the manner of commercial British gunflint technology (Figure 28, e). Although both snapped edges and one lateral edge show slight edge modification on the dorsal surface (small flake scars with step and hinge termini on two edges and feather termini on the third), they barely constitute retouch using the conservative threshold applied in this research. However, the one lateral edge does display slightly more severe modification on the ventral surface, qualifying the specimen as retouched. Small overlapping flake scars with feather termini extend no more than five mm from the edge of origin.

RETOUCHED MICROBLADES

Of the 604 microblades present in the Campus Site collections, only three are retouched. There are no apparent criteria for selecting individual microblades for retouching other than length. Only one specimen is complete, but the other two retouched microblade fragments are relatively long. In all cases retouching occurred on the dorsal surface and lateral edges. Retouch on both lateral edges is present in one case.

RETOUCHED FLAKES

The majority of the retouched specimens in the Campus Site collections are modified flakes, with a total of 137 specimens. Raw material selection was relatively indiscriminant, with types represented in roughly the same frequencies as found in the unmodified flake assemblage: chert (128 specimens, or 93%), obsidian (4 specimens, or 3%), and coarse-grained material with conchoidal fracture (3 specimens, or 3%). Six chert specimens were thermally altered. Selection for larger flakes (to retouch) is evident (Table 12), but support for this statement requires that specimens broken after retouching be distinguished from flake fragments that were subsequently retouched. Specimens with edges formed by flat facets perpendicular to the plane of the artifact were scrutinized to determine whether retouch scars overlap the edge facet or whether the edge facet truncates retouch scars. In instances where the edge facet and the retouch were not adjacent, so that the sequence of operations could not be distinguished, the specimen was considered to be a flake fragment that was subsequently retouched, and hence

Table 12. Descriptive statistics for weight, in grams, of complete retouch specimens and total retouch sample.

Retouch Class	Weight: Total Sample	Weight: Complete Specimens
Macroblade	16.4 mean	20.5 mean
	4.2 min	—
	30.2 max	—
	9.4 SD	—
	6 = N	1 = N
Microblade	0.5 mean	0.7 mean
	0.3 min	—
	0.7 max	—
	0.2 SD	—
	3 = N	1 = N
Flake: short axis retouch	9.5 mean	10.1 mean
	0.5 min	0.5 min
	29.5 max	29.5 max
	6.5 SD	6.8 SD
	43 = N	35 = N
Flake: long axis retouch	26.9 mean	29.9 mean
	6.8 min	6.8 min
	50.3 max	50.3 max
	15.4 SD	14.8 SD
	13 = N	11 = N
Flake: irregular retouch	6.4 mean	9.7 mean
	0.1 min	0.1 min
	37.1 max	37.1 max
	8.2 SD	11.1 SD
	77 = N	24 = N
Flake: misc. retouch	5.6 mean	1.9 mean
	1.9 min	—
	9.2 max	—
	5.2 SD	—
	2 = N	1 = N

complete. Of the total number of retouched flakes, 71 (53%) were complete, and 64 (47%) appear to have been broken after they were retouched. Using these criteria, most of the very small retouched specimens were judged to be incomplete. There is some potential for confusing them with spalls from Donnelly burins, which still retain a portion of the notched platform as a small retouched zone: although burin spalls from Donnelly burins should in theory show a bulb or bulbar scar on the facet of detachment, as is discussed elsewhere a burin spall found to join a Donnelly burin in the Campus Site collection did not display such a distinctive facet.

A visual sort of the retouched flake specimens in the Campus Site produces four categories of artifacts. The first is a group of irregularly shaped flakes and flake fragments that display some portion of retouched edge, but are not retouched to the extent that their original flake (or flake fragment) outline is much altered. The second is a group of large symmetrical complete flakes with long, straight or slightly convex retouched edges on their long axis. The third group consists of artifacts with much of their edge retouched relatively symmetrically into a roughly round or oval shape on their short axis. The fourth (miscellaneous) category consists of a specimen with a quite sharply retouched point, and a specimen with a deeply concave retouched notch.

Although there are a very few retouched specimens that were assigned to one category over another with some reticence, this four-way division is simple, replicable, and describes the most obvious variability in the assemblage. Other researchers have characterized the Campus Site assemblage using somewhat similar divisions and terms such as "side scrapers" and "end scrapers" (Nelson 1937:267–272: Rainey 1939:383), referring to the orientation of the retouch in relation to the proximal end of the flake: end scrapers are retouched on the distal end and side scrapers are retouched on lateral edges. The morphological typology used in this restudy discriminates according to whether the retouch is on the long axis or short axis of the specimen—regardless of the bulb of force orientation.

Irregular Retouched Flakes and Flake Fragments. Seventy-seven specimens are assigned to this category. Most have only one retouched edge segment, although three have two retouched segments. A retouched segment is a length of retouched edge whose end points are marked by a shift to an unmodified edge, an abrupt shift in curvature, or a shift from dorsal to ventral retouch. In this group all orientations—with respect to the original direction of flake removal—are evident, with no overwhelming preference for distal or lateral edges. Dorsal surfaces were retouched almost exclusively. No overwhelming preference for retouching the long or short axis is apparent, when the choice was available. The edge angles of the retouch show a wide range of variability, but most are relatively low—reflecting the thinness of many of the specimens. Chert dominates this category with 72 examples, while two obsidian specimens are present and three specimens are of the coarse material with conchoidal fracture.

Large Symmetrical Flakes with Long Axis Retouch. The thirteen specimens assigned to this category are much longer in one axis than the other, and in all cases it is the longer axis that is significantly retouched. Five specimens have their positive bulb of force on the shorter edge, four specimens have their bulb of force directly on the long axis, and four have their bulbs at an angle to the long axis of the artifact (Figure 31). Modification is almost wholly on the dorsal surface, with only one example showing some minor retouch on the ventral surface in addition to dorsal retouch, apparently to realign the modified edge. All are of chert.

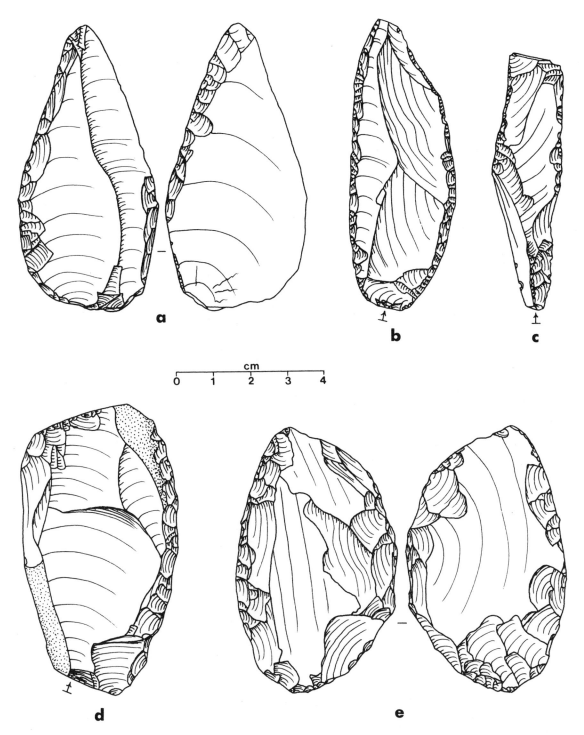

Figure 31. Long-axis retouch. a. (#3-128), b. (#71-4245), c. (#3-164), d. (#66-3264), e. (#3-123).

Symmetrical Flakes with Short Axis Retouch. Assigned to this category are 43 specimens, of which two are of obsidian and the remainder are of chert. Many show considerable bilateral symmetry, with a steeply retouched segment (usually the distal end) flanked by two less steeply retouched segments, at a sharp angle to the steep segment (Figures 32 and 33). Edge angles range from 43 to 83 degrees. The majority of specimens are retouched on their dorsal surface.

Of note are the two obsidian specimens which—in addition to a steeply retouched dorsal surface—have several flakes removed from their ventral surface. Pronounced

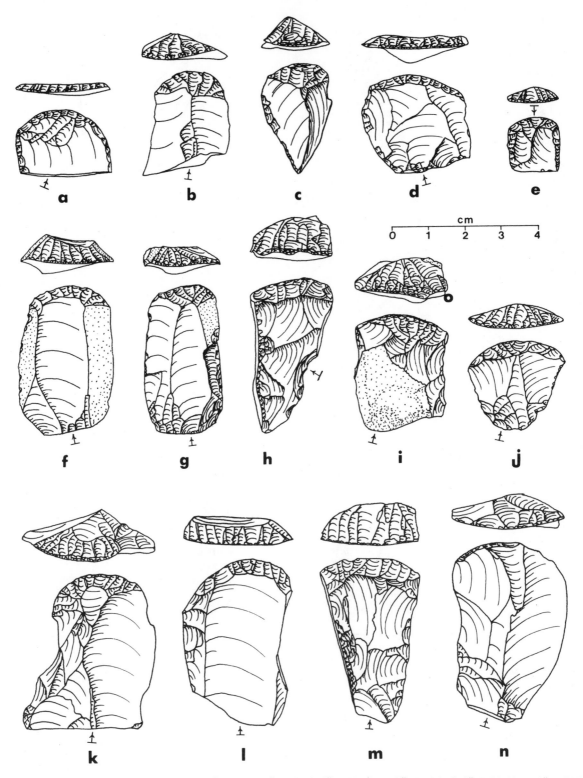

Figure 32. Short-axis retouch. a. (#3-108), b. (#3-86), c. (#3-92), d. (#37-2072), e. (#67-497), f. (#67-2238), g. (#66-987), h. (#3-106), i. (#3-84), j. (#3-87), k. (#67-4478), l. (#3-85), m. (#3–107), n. (#66-4021).

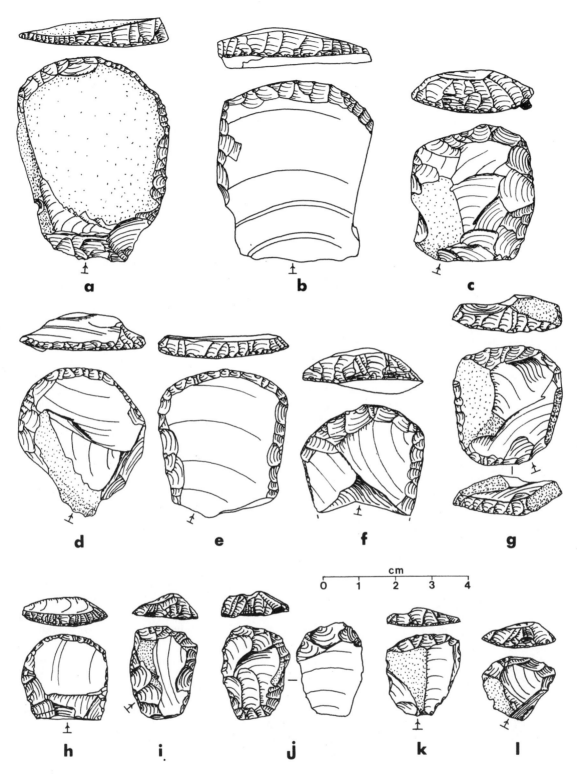

Figure 33. Short-axis retouch. a. (#66-907), b. (#3-103), c. (#3-110), d. (#3-89), e. (#67-2996), f. (#3-101), g. (#3-104), h. (#3-111), i. (#67-491), j. (#67-5208), k. (#67-1347), l. (#3-93).

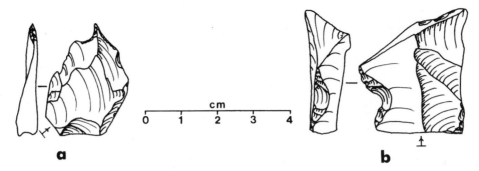

Figure 34. Miscellaneous retouch. a. pointed (#3-348), b. notched (#3-366).

bulbs of force suggest percussion flaking (Figure 32, j). Both have remnants of cortex on their dorsal surface.

Miscellaneous Retouched Flakes.   One artifact displays a distinct point formed by steep retouch on the dorsal surface (Figure 34, a). Two very small, short burin facets emanate from the point. In other typologies such an artifact might be called a "graver" (Holmes 1986:55–70).

Another artifact has been dorsally retouched on one edge to form a deep notch (Figure 33, b). The specimen is a medial flake fragment with a triangular cross section, and appears to have been deliberately snapped, judging from the pronounced cone of force emanating from the dorsal surface at one broken edge.

SUMMARY OF RETOUCHED SPECIMENS

Retouching was applied to flakes, macroblades, and microblades. Of the latter, only three specimens were recovered. Half of the twelve macroblades were retouched. For both microblades and macroblades retouching was restricted to the dorsal surface; lateral edges were preferred in all cases except for one macroblade, on which the distal end was retouched. A single snapped medial macroblade fragment has the appearance of a gunflint.

The sample size of unifacially retouched flakes is much larger, and there is more variability. More than half of them are flakes and flake fragments, with little modification other than retouch on a portion of one edge; the specimens have no symmetry and instead retain their original irregular flake form. Of the more symmetrical specimens, the dominant form (which in conventional typologies would be termed "endscraper") has retouch on the short axis. These specimens tend to be relatively small, while specimens with retouch on the long axis (which are less frequent in the collection), are larger. Two unifacially retouched forms represented by one specimen each are a flake fragment with a deep notch flaked into one edge on the dorsal surface, and a flake with a distinct sharp retouched point. Retouching done on specimens as preparation for burination is considered in the burin section.

Burin Technology

The term burin is now firmly associated with the Campus site assemblage, but this was not always the case. Neither Nelson (1937) or Rainey (1939) noted them in the collections, and it was not until the 1950s that burins and burin spalls of any sort were systematically described from Alaskan contexts (Giddings 1951, 1956). Irving (1955) focused specifically on specimens from Alaska's interior, identifying two burins and a burin spall from the Campus site. Flakes with burin facets originating from retouched margins, termed Donnelly burins, were later identified from the Campus Site and described as a diagnostic artifact of the Denali Complex by West (1967:369). The most intensive analysis of burins in the Campus Site collection has been by Mauger (1970), although he considered only Donnelly burins.

Burin technology involves the process of removing the edge of a piece of stone, using force applied parallel rather than perpendicular to the edge. Almost any sort of chipped stone artifact (excluding large blocky specimens) can be subjected to burination, but the most common burins are made on flakes and bifaces. Burination creates two classes of artifacts: burins and burin spalls.

Burins are those specimens which have had an edge removed through burination. They are identified by a long negative flake scar forming the specimen's edge, with undulations indicating that force was applied in a direction parallel to the specimen's edge. These burin facets, as they are called, are distinct from simple breaks, whether accidental or intentional, although it may be difficult to determine whether the facets result from intentional or accidental burination (Epstein 1963:194). Burination is similar to microblade production, in that the force is applied parallel to the specimen's edge, and a long thin spall is removed that thereby removes the "edge" of the parent specimen, which now becomes a burin. In this analysis burins are generally distinguished from microblade cores in that: (1) burins are less wide than microblade cores, (2) burins have one burin facet per edge, and no more than two, (3) prepared platforms on burins consist of a slight notch formed by unifacial retouch, whereas prepared platforms on most microblade cores are formed by a single flake scar often struck perpendicular to the blade face. A fourth observation, provided by Mauger (1970:20), is that "cores in the Campus collection always have a single blade face while Donnelly burins may have two or three facet areas." In lithic studies using functional in addition to technological and morphological criteria, the existance of wear on the edges of the burin facet is also taken as a discriminating attribute (Mauger 1970:46, Holmes 1986:88).

As might be expected when one is familiar with both technologies, burins and microblade cores are not completely mutually exclusive; there seem to have been times in the decision-making process when the craftsman diverged from one model and chose an option more common to other technologies. Holmes (1986:88) explicitly recognizes this in his Lake Minchumina assemblage, stating that some "flake burins resemble the small microblade cores made on flakes, "Campus-type". . . . technologically and morphologically, these tools clearly overlap." Despite the potential gradation from burins to microblade cores, however, the criteria used for discrimination in this analysis assigned individual artifacts to the same category as was done by previous researchers and catalogers.

A burin spall is the former edge of an artifact after it has been removed through burination. It may be triangular or rectangular in cross-section, with a positive bulb of force at one end. Triangular, or primary, burin spalls are similar to the triangular blades removed from a microblade core, differing in that burin spalls need not have dorsal facets indicating a direction of force parallel to that creating the ventral surface (as microblades would). Furthermore, Pitzer (1977:8–9) states that "burin spalls will more frequently end in hinge fractures," although this is not necessarily implied for the Campus Site sample, based on inspection of the burins. There is also potential for confusing burin spalls—especially triangular ones—with specimens produced in the course of platform preparation and blade face realignment of microblade cores.

Mauger (1970:24) believed that triangular spalls with bifacial retouch on the dorsal surface were from microblade cores, while triangular spalls with unifacial retouch on the dorsal surface are burin spalls. The conservative approach taken in this restudy resulted in few burin spalls being identified in the collections. A rectangular cross section was used as a primary criterion for identification of burin spalls.

Beyond the elementary dichotomy of burins and burin spalls, certain attributes can be used to subdivide burins into smaller subsets. Holmes (1986:81–88), for example, uses such factors as the number of burin facets, the direction of burin spall removal, and the number of platforms, to separate burins into groups. For the Campus Site material the criteria used for grouping are: (1) presence or absence of platform preparation, and (2) whether the bur-

Table 13. Comparison of sample sizes for different platform types and parent specimens of burins.

	Flake	Biface	Retouch
Prepared Platform	22	3	1
Unprepared Platform	4	1	1

Table 14. Descriptive statistics for weight of Donnelly burins, in grams.

Donnelly burins (N = 22)	4.5 mean
	0.6 min
	24.0 max
	5.3 SD

inated specimen is an otherwise unmodified flake, a biface, or a retouched specimen (Table 13).

Donnelly Burins. The sample of burinated flakes with prepared platforms have been termed "Donnelly burins," after the Donnelly Ridge site which produced the first described examples (West 1967:369). Informally, specialists in interior Alaska prehistory continue to debate the form and function of such specimens; investigators who employ more detailed typologies for burinated flakes sometimes reserve the term "Donnelly burin" only for those with multiple facets around the perimeter of the flake. Much of this discussion about Donnelly burins draws on an unpublished study by Mauger (1970), who used several data sources to analyze Campus Site specimens from the University of Alaska Museum collection. Following his approach, the manufacturing sequence is used to organize the information.

The Donnelly burins are of fine-grained siliceous material: no obsidian specimens are present. By definition, all the Donnelly burins are on flakes. Some selection for flake size is evident, as the range in weight for burins is narrower than that for all unmodified flakes (Table 14). Donnelly burins were not manufactured on very small or very large flakes.

Mauger (1970:24) stated that "unifacially retouched triangular spalls . . . are initial spalls from Donnelly burins." Whether or not these initial burin spalls can be accurately discriminated from similar artifacts associated with microblade cores, it is likely that the unmodified margin of the stone was first strengthened and aligned to help create a uniform and straight burin facet. A shallow notch was then unifacially (and steeply) retouched adjacent to the intended burin facet to provide a platform of suitable angle and strength to allow removal of the burin spall (Figure 35). Crushing of the flake scars in the retouched notch is considered a function of manufacture rather than use (although, again, some researchers would privately disagree), while truncation of the flake scars in

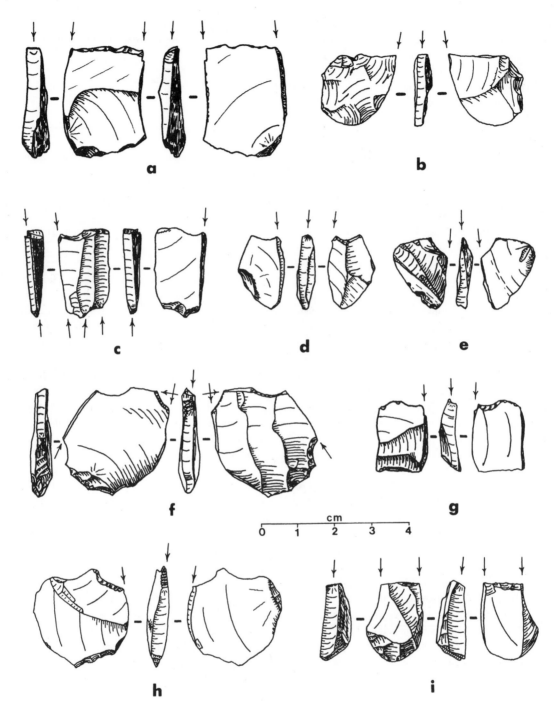

Figure 35. Burins. a., c–i. Donnelly burins (#3-74, #66-160, #3-8, #3-78, #66-3699, #3-169, #3-83, #3-73), b. burinated flake with unprepared platform (#66-3021).

the retouched notch by the burin facet indicates that the notch was definitely created prior to burination (Mauger 1970:32, 25).

A burin spall joining a Donnelly burin helps illustrate the process of burin spall removal (Figure 36, b). In this case a medial flake fragment was retouched on opposing edges, one dorsally and one ventrally. The ventrally re-

touched segment served as a platform, and a burin spall (Figure 36, c) was removed. The burin facet so created was then used as a platform from which to remove more burin spalls, indicated by one complete and one incomplete burin facet on the burin. Interestingly, the ventral surface of the recovered burin spall, and the corresponding burin facet on the burin, are difficult to identify as the

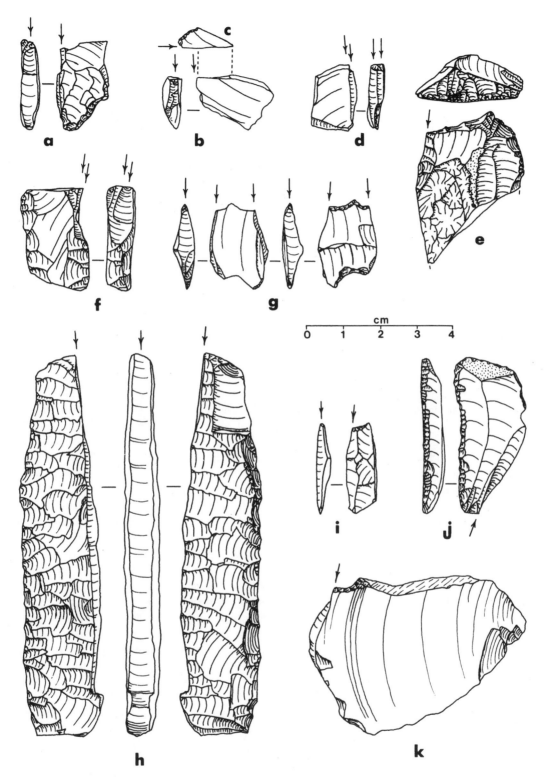

Figure 36. Burins. a., b., d., g., i., k. Donnelly burins (#3-80, #67-3010, #3-69, #67-785, #3-79, #67-3200), c. burin spall (#67-3101), e., j. burinated retouched specimens (#3-98, #3-119), f., h. burinated bifaces (#3-61, #67-1383).

result of burination rather than a snap. Inspection of the few burin spalls in the collection indicates that in two cases the dorsal surface of the spalls appear to reflect a snap fracture. This could indicate a conscious production mode in which the initial burin spall is prepared for removal by snapping the flake, thereby creating a straight edge to help guide the force removing the burin spall.

Despite the lack of ripples on the burin facets of archaeological specimens, replication and experimentation by Mauger (1970:26–27) led him to propose that direct percussion, rather than indirect percussion or pressure, was used to remove the burin spall on Donnelly burins from the Campus Site. This was inferred by the difficulty in avoiding hinge and step terminations in experimental contexts, using indirect percussion or pressure, compared to the ease with which direct percussion produced feathered terminations that created a complete burin facet along the edge of the burin. Most of the Donnelly burins from the Campus Site display complete burin facets.

Several Donnelly burins from the Campus Site exhibit more than one notch or more than one burin facet. Expediency is the explanation for this variability provided by Mauger (1970:28). A single notch, at the corner of a specimen, provides a platform for removing burin spalls on two edges of the burin, at right angles to each other. Because an existing straight burin facet provides an excellent guide for subsequent burin spall removals, an exhausted notch might be abandoned in favor of a new notch at the opposite end of the existing burin facet, creating a burin facet with remnants of a notch at each end. Each of these alternatives may sometimes be more efficient than starting at the beginning and going through the whole sequence of edge alignment, notch construction, primary spall removal, etc. The Donnelly burins in the Campus Site collection include the following morphologies: a. one notch and facet (13 examples), b. two sets, each consisting of a notch and a facet (3 examples), c. two opposed notches and one facet (1 example), d. two sets, each consisting of two opposed notches and one facet (3 examples), e. one notch and facet and two opposed notches and one facet (2 examples).

Burinated Flakes (With Unprepared Platforms).

Identification of these artifacts as intentionally burinated is tenuous, due to their lack of prepared platforms and other indications of purposeful alteration. All four specimens would otherwise be classed as flakes, except for a single burin facet on one edge, emanating from an unretouched facet. In one case the burin facet twists over well onto the face of the flake, in two others the burin facet hinges less than 1.0 cm from its proximal end, and only in the fourth (Figure 35, b), does the facet extend along the entire edge, perpendicular to the axis of the flake.

Burinated Bifaces.

Four bifaces in the Campus Site collection display a burin facet. None of the burin facets originate from a bifacially worked point, although this is not necessarily proof that the scars did not result from impact fractures (Epstein 1963, Barton and Bergman 1982:240, Bergman and Newcomer 1983:240–243). Three of the specimens have their burin facets originating from a worked edge (considered to be a prepared platform), while the fourth specimen has a burin facet originating from a snap fracture facet. All the specimens are of chert.

Irving (1955) illustrated and discussed two of these burinated bifaces (Figures 26, a; 36, f), including the one with an unprepared platform. The latter appears to be the medial fragment of a biface (Figure 35, f). Although the burin has been recently damaged, two burin facets are apparent, both originating from this same platform. Both spalls hinged about half-way down the bifacial edge, while a third, possible burin blow was thwarted by a crystalized inclusion near the platform.

Of the three bifacial burins with prepared platforms, the least distinctive is a small, thick trapezoidally shaped specimen with a single burin facet forming one edge. A second specimen (Figure 26, a) is small with a lanceolate form and a burin facet originating from what would be a basal corner. The burin facet extends for a third of the edge, and twists its plane about 90 degrees from its proximal to its distal end. Irving (1955:381) identifies this specimen as a burin "with some reservation," and it remains questionable in this current restudy. The facet could be a perverse fracture accidentally executed in an attempt to further thin the base of the point.

The fourth burinated biface is one of the more spectacular artifacts in the Campus Site collections (Figure 36, h). This long, narrow biface is well made, with parallel flaking over much of its surface. One end of the biface is snapped, the other—where the burin facets originated—is steeply retouched. The retouch was the last alteration of the specimen, as it removed the proximal portion of the burin facet and the proximal portion of a large, regular flake scar that also originated from that end and carried over onto the face of the biface. The burin facet extends almost the length of one edge, for a distance of 9.0 cm, finally hinging 1.0 cm short of the end. Nor was it the first such extensive facet, because the distal remnant of a prior burin facet forms that last 1.0 cm of the edge. Thus the last burin spall detached from the artifact must have been quite rectangular in cross section. The length of the burin facet would imply percussion or indirect percussion as the method of executing the burin blow; it is not suggested to be the result of an impact fracture.

Burinated Retouched Specimens.

Artifacts assigned to this category differ from Donnelly burins, which by definition have retouched platforms for burin spall removal, in that other portions of the artifacts' margins are significantly retouched. There are two specimens in the Campus Site collections, of which one has a retouched platform and the other does not. The latter example (Figure 36, j) was illustrated and discussed by Rainey (1939:384) and Irving (1955), the latter of whom called the specimen a "lamellar gouge" and "flake gouge," but said also that "a case could be made for calling it a burin" (which is probably why he included it in his article on burins). The artifact is of obsidian, although Irving (1955:382) called it black chert, perhaps because of its heavy patination. The dorsal surface of the artifact displays some cortex, and remnants of parallel flake scars predating the artifact's detachment from the core. One margin of the artifact has regular retouch on the dorsal surface, forming a slightly concave edge. A single burin facet originates from the platform of the flake, extending onto the dorsal surface with a 50-degree twist.

The second specimen (Figure 36, e) is of chert, and displays a rich red coloration and two "pot-lids" indicating thermal alteration. Steep retouch extends around 35% of the distal edge on the dorsal surface, conforming to the "end-scraper" form. One end of this retouched edge served as the platform from which the burin spall was forced off, leaving a burin facet 2.1 cm long.

SUMMARY OF BURIN TECHNOLOGY

Burinated flakes, bifaces, and retouched specimens are well represented in the Campus Site collection. Chert was almost always preferred for burins, the one exception being an obsidian specimen. A few burin spalls in the collection imply that the artifacts were burinated at the site. The samples of burinated flakes, bifaces, and retouched specimens each contain some specimens displaying a platform specifically prepared for the burin removal, and some specimens lacking such preparation. The most common burin type in the Campus Site collection is the Donnelly burin—a flake with one or more concavities retouched on its edge to serve as a platform for burin removal.

Miscellaneous Stone Artifacts

Several minor artifact categories in the Campus Site collection have received little attention, perhaps due to their small sample sizes or lack of morphological complexity. Miscellaneous stone artifacts include unaltered cobbles and pebbles, hammerstones, cobble spalls, ground and pitted stones, and tabular slabs.

UNALTERED COBBLES AND PEBBLES

Numerous unmodified pebbles and six cobbles were recovered in the Campus Site excavations and cataloged into the collections. The pebbles may or may not be naturally present in the soil matrix, but the cobbles definitely have their geologic occurrence elsewhere. The pebbles were not analyzed in this study, except for one mentioned below. The cobbles are not unlike hammerstones in their size and raw material, except that they display no battered surfaces. Chert and the coarse-grained material with conchoidal fracture are both represented. The one specimen that may be culturally modified is a thermally fractured cobble, which in other assemblages might be termed "fire-cracked rock."

A small (0.7 g), colorful pebble is likely a manuport. A bedding plane divides the pebble in half; one half is bright red, and the other is a very glossy white. There is no indication of cultural modification, but the stone is inherently conspicuous and emminently collectable.

HAMMERSTONES

Cobbles with battered surfaces are termed hammerstones (Figure 23, f, g). Battering produces crushed and pocked surfaces, or in more severe instances it may create numerous step and hinge fractures that leave large flake scars on the cobble. Both levels of wear are evident on the four specimens in the collection.

COBBLE SPALLS

Cobble spalls are present in the Campus Site collections. These are large primary decortication flakes that lack an obvious platform where force could be easily directed obliquely to the plane of the flake, and display instead at the point of impact crushed surfaces where the dorsal surface meets the ventral surface at an acute angle. Experimentation has shown that striking a hammerstone against an anvil or other hard surface will produce such flakes without platforms (Mobley 1982:96). Of the three examples present, only the largest is further modified, in this case by retouch and a battered edge (Figure 23, d).

GROUND AND PITTED STONES

Few artifacts in the Campus Site collection can be termed ground stone tools. One such specimen appears to be a medial fragment of what was at one time an ovoid siltstone biface (Figure 23, e). Bifacial knapping has helped shape the piece, but subsequent grinding has partially obliterated the flake scar arrises in several places.

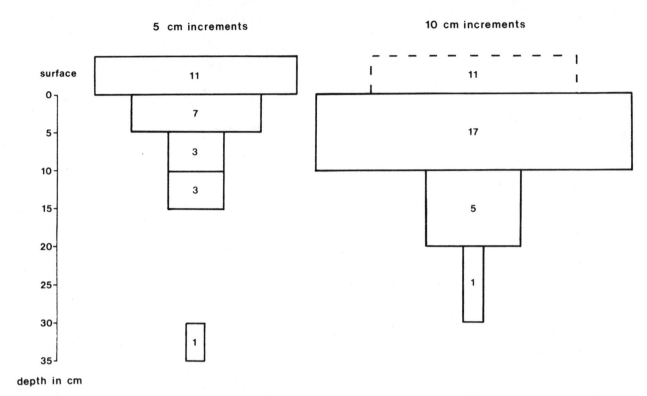

Figure 37. Diagram showing vertical distribution of historic trash (N = 48), according to differing vertical increments used. Note that surface specimens are figured twice.

A tabular rock, with a half-moon or "ulu" shape, has a few flake scars on its margin but not enough to definitely suggest cultural chipping. However, the specimen does have three small pits, one on one side and two on the other, that are likely of cultural origin. Each pit is located very near the center of its respective side, and is 2 mm in diameter and about 1 mm deep. The pits are quite circular, suggesting that they were formed with a rotary motion, and the stone may have served as a bearing for a drill of some kind.

A third groundstone specimen (Figure 23, j), is a fist-sized piece of reddened, vesicular rock, probably classifiable as scoria or pumice. Over a dozen shallow grooves, ranging up to 4.5 cm long, have been worn into the rock. The grooves are U-shaped, with a maximum width of 3.5 mm. Such characteristics would warrant the functional term "abrader" for the tool.

TABULAR SLABS

Several pieces of tabular rock were recovered from the site and cataloged into the collections. These four specimens are of a shale-like material (some may be of the local schist bedrock), that would not show cultural modification very well. All but one appear culturally unaltered. The exception is a large specimen which is bifacially retouched into a semicircular or "D" shape (Figure 23, a). The straight edge is not worked, but rather consists of a naturally flat facet.

SUMMARY OF MISCELLANEOUS STONE ARTIFACTS

Miscellaneous stone artifacts constitute less than 0.1% of the total Campus Site collection, but they help document the range of tool variability present. Unaltered pebbles are the most numerous of this diverse artifact group, with 39 specimens. The remainder—unmodified cobbles, hammerstones, cobble spalls, ground and pitted stones, and tabular slabs—are represented by only a few specimens each (Table 5).

Historic Trash

The Campus Site collections contains a few items (48 specimens) of historic trash, all dating to within the last 80 years. Most of this material consists of rusted nails, some as much as 15 cm in length. A few pieces of window and bottle glass were recovered. Bits of a hard, brittle, dark black material are likely the remains of burned rubber tires (see Figure 38). Folded pieces of rusty ¼-inch mesh screen recovered in 1966 and 1967 are probably remnants from the excavations of the 1930s, subsequently backfilled and inadvertently exposed 30 years later when excavations strayed out of virgin units.

The low sample size for historic trash provides little basis for inferring horizontal patterning. Generally, the density of historic trash increases upslope to the northwest; the four quadrants of Unit N-3 contained 22 specimens, or 46% of the total sample. There is no evidence to suggest that the presence or absence of historic trash in any units is the result of differential collection or curation policies. Hosley and Mauger (1967:5) imply some horizontal pattern of historic trash at the site, stating that the site's "outer limits have been extensively disturbed", with further note of "iron nails being found in direct association with microblades." Five historic specimens have no recorded horizontal provenience.

In those units where historic trash was present, the vertical distribution was recorded in five or ten cm increments (Figure 37). Both sets of data show the majority of the subsurface trash to occur in the uppermost (0–5 cm or 0–10 cm) level, with 23% of the material recovered on the site's surface. Equally notable is the recovery of a specimen at a depth of 30–35 cm. Implications of the spatial distribution of historic trash are discussed in the discussion on dating.

FAUNA

Rainey (1939:382) noted the lack of "habitation refuse" uncovered in the early Campus site excavations, but mentioned the recovery of bone fragments. From the 1966 excavations "some burned and calcined bone was obtained" (Hosley and Mauger 1967:6), and more was collected in 1967. These bone specimens were included in the Campus Site collections obtained on loan, and were scrutinized by John E. Lobdell: the description here is developed from his identifications.

Most of the faunal material consists of small burned and calcined bone fragments, of which the majority are unprovenienced and probably derived from the 1930s excavations. Of the approximately 600 grams of bone present, only about 36 grams was recovered in the 1966 and 1967 excavations. The bone was scattered horizontally throughout many of the excavation units, while vertically it was concentrated between the depths of 5 and 25 cm. The specimens are whitish-grey in color; some are brittle and some are chalky. This material is considered to be culturally modified by burning, as opposed to several lots of small mammal bone which are quite intact and considered to be recent intrusions. The culturally modified specimens suggest deliberate processing for the purpose of making bone grease—a food item (Leechman 1951). In some prehistoric sites, disintegrated dog feces can be a source of small bone fragments, especially of small animals, but this would not explain the calcification of the Campus Site specimens, and no indication of canids in the site are present except for a single bone that could just as well represent a wild wolf.

Despite their fragmented and burned condition, some bone specimens are identifiable as to family, genus, or species. A "bison leg bone from UA Campus" (Accession #64–84) was mentioned in University of Alaska-Fairbanks Museum correspondence on file from 1969, but the specimen has been lost and its identification has not been confirmed (it may have been recovered elsewhere on the university grounds). Specimens identified by Lobdell are presented in Table 15. They are listed by animal and by lot—which in this case means the contents of individ-

Table 15. Faunal assemblage from the Campus Site collections, grouped according to accessioned lot.

Taxon	Specimens	Comment
Ursus sp.	2+	bear, cultural
Castor canadensis	8+	beaver, cultural
Castor canadensis	7	beaver, cultural
Castor canadensis	29+	beaver, cultural
Lepus americanus	1	hare, cultural
Lepus americanus	5 maxillae frag.	hare, cultural
Lepus sp.	1 left prox. 1st phalange	hare, cultural
Lepus sp.	2 tibia 8 metapodial 1 phalange 2 calcanii 1 astralagus	hare, intact condition, intrusive
Canis sp.	1	wolf size, cultural
Ungulate	2	bison size, cultural
Ungulate	1 medial femur frag.	bison size, cultural
Ungulate	1 tooth frag.	bison, cultural, buccal surface
Ungulate	1 molar enamel	cultural
Bird	1 synsacrum	cultural
Citellus parryi	almost all elements	Arctic ground squirrel, immature, intrusive

ual vials, specimen boxes, cigar boxes, bottles, etc. Lobdell's comments include the fact that (except for items considered intrusive) no immature animals are represented, size variability suggests more than one beaver present, and in the unidentifiable portion of the fauna assemblage long bone fragments are well represented.

Conclusions to be reached from the faunal assemblage are limited. Hunters at the Campus Site sought and caught both small and large game animals, and—in addition to the meat and other products presumably being utilized—the bones were broken into small fragments and subsequently burned. No exotic species are present in the assemblage.

DATING THE CAMPUS SITE

When Rainey (1939, 1940) and Nelson (1935, 1936) evaluated the Campus Site and its material, they did not have radiocarbon dating as a tool for assessing its chronological placement. Using typological comparisons, Rainey (1939:388, 1953:43–44) decided that the Campus Site was earlier than Athabascan occupation in Alaska, because copper and organic artifacts were not present. For some time, the absolute dating of the Campus Site was ambiguous; Irving (1955:380) was able to state that "No hypotheses have been advanced as to the actual age of the material."

West (1967:361. 372) recognized the problem also, saying that "Despite the difficulties—principally dating—that have always tended to becloud its significance, the Campus site represents the most important single landmark in the history of interior Alaskan archaeology. . . . [it] has always been difficult to interpret, and its place in American prehistory has remained, to the present day, rather nebulous." He went on to include the Campus Site with the Donnelly Ridge, Teklanika East, and Teklanika West sites in his newly defined Denali Complex, estimated to date from about 15,000 to 10,000 B.P. (West 1967:373, 378). In a subsequent article, West (1975) presented radiocarbon evidence from other sites, in the Tangle Lakes area, suggesting a time span of roughly 12,000 to 8,000 B.P. for the Denali Complex.

Obsidian Hydration Dating

The first absolute date reported for the Campus Site was mentioned by Hans-Georg Bandi, who personally witnessed excavations there in 1967 (Figure 6). He states that "by measuring the hydration layer of some obsidian flakes Y. Katsui obtained a date of 8,400 for the Campus site industry" (Bandi 1969:52). West (1981:142) also mentions this date for the Campus Site, but the obsidian hydration rate or other factors used in calculating the date have never been published; the unreliability of single obsidian hydration estimates has been demonstrated by Clark (1984a).

A more recent attempt to date the Campus Site using the obsidian hydration technique is that of John P. Cook, as part of an ongoing project to analyze source areas and hydration rates for all of Alaska's obsidian outcrops (Michels 1984, 1985). Publication is incomplete, but Cook (1975:129) mentions a date of about 3,300 B.P. for the Campus Site, based on five samples. That estimate uses a

hydration rate derived from comparison with the hydration rinds on dated specimens from sites at Healy Lake, however, and does not take into account variability that may be due to different environments or sources of obsidian (Cook, personal communication). Similarly, Holmes (1978) used Healy Lake data and information from samples at Site MMK-4 at Lake Minchumina to suggest a dating range of 4,500 to 1,000 B.P. for the Campus Site, based on obsidian hydration rind measurements.

Radiocarbon Dating Efforts

Prior to the present study, the Campus Site had never been radiocarbon dated. Several reasons can be suggested to explain this: (1) the 1930s excavations were conducted prior to the availability of the technique; (2) the 1960s excavations recovered no organic artifacts, few faunal remains, and mostly small charcoal samples; (3) suggestions that the site was used for the university's freshman bonfires during the 1920s and early 1930s (Figure 38) raised fears of sample contamination (although Al Dickey, who worked at the site in the 1930s, stated in a personal communication to the author that "our dig was thirty or forty feet, I would say, south of the bonfire site"); and (4) funds were not readily available for radiocarbon dating. In 1967, H. Morris Morgan—who supervised excavations at the Campus Site in 1966—sent a bone sample weighing 30 grams to the radiocarbon laboratories of the University of Pennsylvania, but the sample was judged much too small for processing. It is not clear from the records or the collections if that sample was returned.

However, the bone and charcoal samples that were recovered from the 1966 and 1967 excavations were curated with the artifact collections of the University of Alaska-Fairbanks Museum, and the Canadian Museum of Civilization. These samples were acquired on loan, and locational data on each was put into the university computer to help organize them and select likely ones for radiocarbon processing. Objects of the dating program were to assess whether the site is multicomponent, and assign the component(s) an absolute date. To do this, it was necessary that radiocarbon dates sample a range of depths and areas within the site. The samples were ranked according to size, depth, and horizontal location, and as funds were acquired, selected samples were submitted for processing.

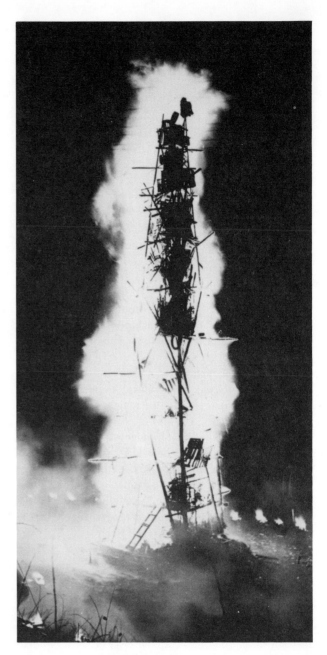

Figure 38. The freshman bonfire of 1928. (Charles Bunnell photographs #55-1026-2 and #58-1026-3, Archives of the University of Alaska Fairbanks).

Samples were submitted for dating over several years through the support of: Albert Dickey, Alaska Heritage Research Group, Alaska Division of Geological and Geophysical Surveys, Bureau of Land Management-Fairbanks, and Alaska Historical Commission. Two different laboratories conducted the radiocarbon analysis. Dicarb Radioisotope Co., of Gainesville, Florida, processed two samples, and the remainder were handled by Beta Analytic, Inc., of Coral Gables, Florida.

RADIOCARBON DATING RESULTS

Of the charcoal and bone samples submitted to radiocarbon laboratories for inspection, some were rejected immediately as unsuitable for processing. Two samples were lost by the U.S. Postal Service in Express Mail between Anchorage and Coral Gables, and never recovered. Of those which were processed, four (DIC-2794, BETA-7223, BETA-7074, BETA-4259) yielded insufficient carbon for a date (Table 16). The remaining samples are

Table 16. Uncalibrated results of the radiocarbon samples, and their vertical and horizontal location in the site.

LABORATORY #	SAMPLE #	LOCATION	RESULT
DIC-2793	66–9019	5–10 cm, Unit NW I7	Modern
DIC-2794	66–9014	10–15 cm, Unit NE H5	insufficient carbon
Beta-10879	67–2225	10–15 cm, Unit SE L5	650 ± 200 B.P.
	67–2237	10–15 cm, Unit SE L5	
	67–3046	10–15 cm, Unit SW L6	
	67–3047	10–15 cm, Unit SW L6	
	67–3048	10–15 cm, Unit SW L6	
Beta-4260	66–9030	15–20 cm, Unit NW G7	2860 ± 180 B.P.
Beta-7075	67–4334	20–25 cm, Unit NE K5	2725 ± 125 B.P.
	67–4677	20–25 cm, Unit SW K5	
	67–3784	20–25 cm, Unit NW K5	
Beta-10878	66–9027	20–25 cm, Unit SW H6	40 ± 110 B.P.
Beta-7224	67–1566	20–30 cm, Unit SW N3	240 ± 120 B.P.
Beta-6829	67–1936	20–30 cm, Unit SW O4	3500 ± 140 B.P.
Beta-7223	67–4381	25–30 cm, Unit NE K5	insufficient carbon
no #	67–5022	25–30 cm, Unit SW K5	lost in transit
no #	67–4854	25–30 cm, Unit SW K5	lost in transit
Beta-7074	67–3558	25–30 cm, Unit NE K5	insufficient carbon
	67–5112	25–30 cm, Unit NW L5	
	67–2340	30–35 cm, Unit SE L5	
	67–2640	30–35 cm, Unit SW L5	
Beta-4259	67–4031	35–40 cm, Unit NW K5	insufficient carbon

discussed individually in their vertical order, using uncalibrated results.

The shallowest charcoal specimen dated was CS66–9019, from the 5–10 cm level of Unit NW17. As with almost all the charcoal samples submitted, the specimen was small and contained numerous rootlets. It yielded a date of Modern (laboratory specimen number DIC-2793), the specific activity being 2% greater than the 1950 standard set by international convention.

A bone sample was assembled from specimens with five different accession numbers (CS67–2225, CS67–2237, CS67–3046, CS67–3047, CS67–3048), all consisting of small friable specimens from the 10–15 cm level of the site. Horizontally, the samples came from Unit SEL5 or the adjoining Unit SWL6. Combination of several bone samples was necessary to provide sufficient volume for dating using an AMS (particle accelerator) process. Care was taken to limit the vertical variability to one five-cm increment, and the horizontal variability to two adjoining units. The sample was given the laboratory number of BETA-10879, and yielded a date of 650 +/− 200 B.P.

The next sample in vertical order was CS66–9030, consisting of charcoal from the 15–20 cm level of Unit NWG7. A date of 2,860 +/− 180 B.P. was obtained from the sample, given the laboratory number of BETA-4260. Again the sample was small, resulting in the large statistical error.

Three charcoal samples were combined to provide a sufficient sample size for BETA-7075. Samples CS67–4334, CS67–4677, and CS67–3784 were all from the 20–25 cm level, but from three different quadrants of the K5 unit. The date obtained from the combined samples was 2,725 +/− 125 B.P.

A small charcoal sample from the 20–25 cm level in the central portion of the site (Unit SWH6) was chosen for dating by the AMS process. The sample's accession number was CS66–9027, and its processing number became BETA-10878. A date of 40 +/− 110 B.P. was obtained.

Two horizontally separated charcoal samples from the 20–30 cm level were processed individually. Specimen CS67–1566 from Unit SWN3 was processed as BETA-7224, yielding a date of 240 +/− 120 B.P. A date of 3,500 +/− 140 B.P. (BETA-6829) was yielded by charcoal specimen CS67–1936 from Unit SWO4.

Interpretation of the Radiocarbon Dating

Not all the radiocarbon samples seem to reflect aboriginal occupation, as several are recent. A date simply termed "Modern" was derived for DIC-2793, from the 5–10 cm level of the site. Deeper in the deposit at the 20–25 cm level, BETA-10878 yielded a date of 40 +/− 110 B.P. Finally, from the 20–30 cm level, a date of 240 +/− 120 was obtained for BETA-7224. This date (on a bone sample) is also essentially modern, as expanding the error to two standard deviations provides a bracketing date range with an upper limit of 1950 A.D. All three of these samples may represent early university activity such as the freshman bonfires of the 1920s and 1930s, which must

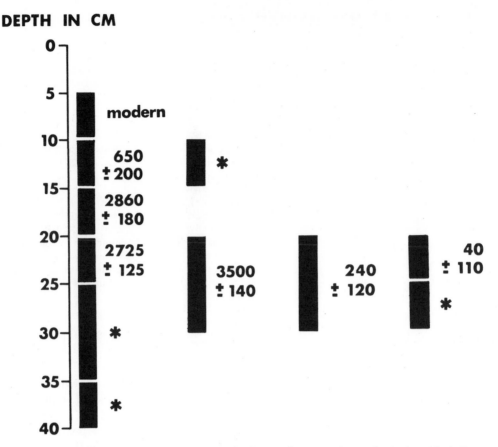

Figure 39. Radiocarbon samples processed from the Campus Site, according to depth. Asterisks indicate samples with insufficient carbon.

have produced considerable charcoal (Figure 38). The presence of such recent dates in vertical contexts down to the 20–30 cm level, in separated areas of the site, implies subsequent soil disturbance in at least some parts of the Campus Site. The vertical distribution of modern trash (excluding that resulting from the 1930s excavations) confirms limited soil disturbance (Figure 37).

The goal of sampling a range of vertical and horizontal areas within the Campus Site was partially met. It should be remembered that specimens were available only from that portion of the site excavated in 1966 and 1967; no charcoal was collected during earlier or later excavations. The dated samples are distributed broadly across the site (see Figure 41). No charcoal samples or large bone samples were recovered from Units I1, J0, or K1, so radiocarbon dating was not possible there. The remainder of the site is broadly represented. There is little correlation between the horizontal location of the samples and their dates—the 3,500 B.P. date is somewhat near the 240 B.P. date, and the Modern date is more-or-less between the 2,725 B.P. and 2,860 B.P. dates.

The vertical distribution of dates is not quite so unpatterned (Figure 39). The most shallow sample—from the

5–10 cm level—did yield a modern date, which is in accord with an intact stratigraphy. Below that a sample from the 10–15 cm level yielded a date of 650 +/− 200 B.P., which is also in correct stratigraphic order. The samples from the 15–20 cm and 20–25 cm increments have overlapping standard deviations and can be considered contemporaneous at about 2,800 B.P. A sample from the 20–30 cm level dated older, to 3,500 B.P. These dates increase in age as the depth increases, suggesting that the arbitrary 5 and 10 cm level excavation increments have some vertical integrity. The two recent dates (240 +/− 120 B.P., and 40 +/− 110 B.P.), are out of stratigraphic order, however. Charcoal samples from the 25–30 cm, 25–35 cm, and 35–40 cm level were submitted for dating, but were destroyed in the process of discovering that they were too small for regular radiocarbon assay. These would have provided dates for the deepest portions of the site deposit, but, unfortunately, no portion of those samples was set aside for possible AMS processing (as is now the policy of the laboratory), and no other samples are available from those depths in the site. To summarize, using the samples available from the 1966 and 1967 excavations, and sampling a range of horizontal and vertical variability, no charcoal or other organic material from the Campus Site could be found to date older than 3,500 years B.P.

Spatial Analysis of Artifact Distribution

The horizontal and vertical positions of artifacts bear on the number of components present at the Campus Site, which is a question associated with that of absolute dating. Because of the lack of features and visible natural stratigraphy, components must be isolated on the basis of artifacts and their distribution, as well as radiocarbon dates. As mentioned earlier, horizontal and vertical provenience is available only from the more recent excavations. Stated simply, the question is whether particular kinds of artifacts are concentrated at certain depths or in certain areas of the site.

Microblade technology has been singled out as a major characteristic of the Denali Complex, as opposed to core/flake technology and biface manufacture—which have a

much wider temporal range. Microblades, flakes, and bifaces were found at all depths in the Campus Site deposit, with sample sizes sufficient for graphic comparison. It is useful to evaluate the collection in 5 cm increments, since this was the finest vertical increment used and over 75% of the sample is recorded on that scale.

VERTICAL DISTRIBUTION OF ARTIFACTS

A graph of microblades in each vertical level shows that most of the microblades were recovered between 10–25 cm in depth (Figure 40). Above and below that depth the number of microblades drops markedly, and gradually decreases through the remaining levels. The same pattern occurs in the vertical distribution of flake debris and biface thinning flakes. In fact, the relative percentage of microblades, flake debris, and biface thinning flakes covary within a narrow range in each vertical level. The 35–40 cm and 40–45 cm levels are exceptions but are not significant, the former because it suffers from very small

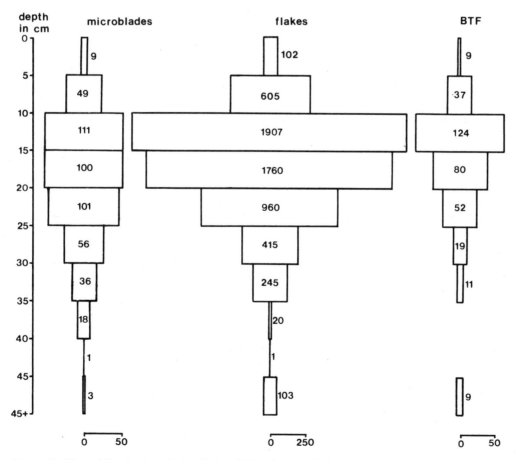

Figure 40. Vertical distribution of microblades, flake debris, and biface thinning flakes in the Campus Site. Numbers in or beside the bars indicate sample sizes.

sample sizes. In the case of the 40–45 cm level, the sample sizes are artificially increased because of computer coding procedures in which the final vertical increment consisted of everything below 45 cm. Due to a slightly undulating contact between the soil and underlying bedrock, there were a few places in the site where artifacts were recovered at depths deeper than 50 cm relative to the immediate ground surface, thus differentially augmenting the sample size of the final vertical increment as it was coded for this analysis. Excluding the 35–40 cm and 45+ cm levels, the vertical distribution pattern is one in which microblades consistently form between 5% and 12% of each five cm level's assemblage, biface thinning flakes contribute 4% to 8%, and flake debris comprises between 88% and 95%.

Two possible explanations for this pattern can be suggested. The first is that the cultural material originated from one major depositional event, on a land surface now buried between 10 and 25 cm below the modern ground surface. Subsequent soil movements dispersed the artifacts vertically from the original depositional plane, upward to near the surface and downward to below 35 cm. A second explanation is that the soil has accumulated more or less continuously, incorporating cultural material from successive occupations along the way, so that those artifacts recovered from 30–35 cm in depth are older than those from the 10–15 cm level (which in turn are older than those found within 0–5 cm of the surface). The issue becomes whether the soil matrix has vertical integrity, and—if so—how much. The evidence does not conclusively favor either hypothesis.

That there may have been upward and downward movement of artifacts is suggested by the discovery of ice wedge casts elsewhere on the university grounds (Péwé 1965b:13–14), the former plowing of the nearby land surface, and the observation during excavation of vertically oriented artifacts within the site matrix (Hosley and Mauger 1967:4). An ice wedge cast was tentatively identified directly in the Campus Site matrix during the excavations of 1966, but the excavators were hesitant to confirm them as such; ice wedge casts would be more likely found in the underlying broken schist, in any case. Cryoturbation has been noted as a significant site formation process elsewhere in Alaska's interior, such as the Dry Creek site (Wood and Johnson 1978:370). According to inspection of aerial photographs, plowing of the university property early in the campus's history extended up to the brow of the hill, but apparently did not extend down to include the entire archaeological deposit (Figures 3 and 4). The presence of vertically-oriented artifacts may to some extent be indicative of soil disturbance subsequent to cultural deposition, but a certain rate of incidence would be expected due to simple probability. The vertical distribution of historic trash, which was originally deposited very near if not at the excavation surface, shows some movement in the site matrix (Figure 37).

Arguing against the idea that only one major depositional event is represented in the deposit, are the facts that the radiocarbon dates are more or less in stratigraphic order and can be interpreted as representing two distinct times—around 650 and 3,000 years ago (referring to the three dates between 3,500 +/− 140 and 2,725 +/− 125 B.P.), and that no paleosols were found within the 10–25 cm level. The noted absence of paleosols or living floors is significant, though, since the excavators of the 1930s and 1960s were obviously sensitive to the need for identifying them, (*Farthest North Collegian* 1934, Rainey 1939:381–383, Hosley 1968:2). The identification of paleosols in interior Alaska has been debated for such archaeological contexts as the Chugwater site (Maitland 1986:20–23); development of organic soils in the Fairbanks area is inhibited by the subarctic environmental conditions, in that "organic matter decomposes very slowly, the plants have shallow root systems, and soil mixing fauna are scarce in the region" (DeMent 1962:97). Instead, the soil consists of a thin organic mat overlying unbedded loess deposits, which are only slightly altered to form the Subarctic Brown Forest soil (Péwé 1965b:15–16). The rate of accumulation for this loess at the Campus Site is unknown, as "the loess deposited in Illinoian, Wisconsin, and post-Wisconsin time constitutes one relatively uniform loess layer, and to date it has not been possible to differentiate this loess into layers of separate ages" (Péwé 1965b:10). However, its lack of bedding implies relatively continuous loess deposition through time, perhaps up to and including the recent Holocene when the Campus Site was occupied one or more times.

To reject the radiocarbon dates as evidence of two major cultural deposits requires either that one or more samples be judged of natural origin from such phenomena as forest fires, or that some be considered simply wrong due to contamination or statistical uncertainty. The date of 650 +/− 200 B.P. may be suspect simply because it was from a bone sample. Forest fires are not uncommon today in central Alaska, and likely occurred in the past as well. Arguing against a forest fire origin for the Campus Site charcoal samples is their distribution—the specimens were not uniformly present in all excavation units but were instead concentrated in a few areas. Also, no carbonized bark specimens were noted, nor did any of the completely carbonized samples have any morphology betraying a small limb size, as if sticks of all sizes were consumed by a fire and then left undisturbed, as a forest fire might do. Al Dickey (personal communication), when asked about the possibility, stated that he observed nothing in the original excavations of the 1930s to suggest evidence for a forest fire. Nonetheless, the possibility that some of the dated charcoal specimens reflect a forest fire

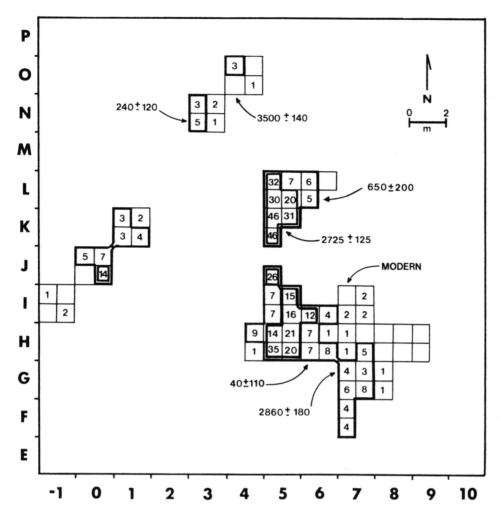

Figure 41. Horizontal distribution of dated samples and microblades, with the microblade frequencies per unit plotted, all levels combined. Units are designated in the text according to the individual (north/south, east/west) quadrant within each 2 m × 2 m area; i.e., NWK1.

cannot be completely discounted; if in direct contact with artifacts, a dated forest fire could still help date the site. Contamination also cannot be ruled out as a possibility, since the specimens were stored in various environments for almost twenty years before processing, but no obvious post-excavation sources of contamination were identified. The potential for modern contamination, especially from the college bonfires, is the most likely explanation for the modern radiocarbon dates. It is difficult to justify singling out any one date and challenging its validity based on the possibility of statistical error.

HORIZONTAL DISTRIBUTION OF ARTIFACTS

The analysis of horizontal variability at the Campus Site is restricted to that information resulting from the 1966 and 1967 excavations, using the grid system established for plotting recovered artifacts. Patterned variability in the horizontal distribution of certain artifact classes (those with high sample sizes) is apparent, with the highest concentrations of debris and microblades present in the central portion (Figures 41 and 42). The way artifact patterns vary horizontally within depth increments has a possible bearing on the number of occupations inferred for the site. If the arbitrary vertical levels reflect a sequence of different occupations, then expected artifact distributions would not be the same from level to level, because it is unlikely that the same specific activities would be practiced in the same restricted areas with the same intensities for occupation after occupation. Conversely, if natural processes have acted on a single distribution pattern, then expected horizontal patterns would be more similar from level to level on the assumption that soil movements would operate on all artifact classes uniformly in each horizontal unit.

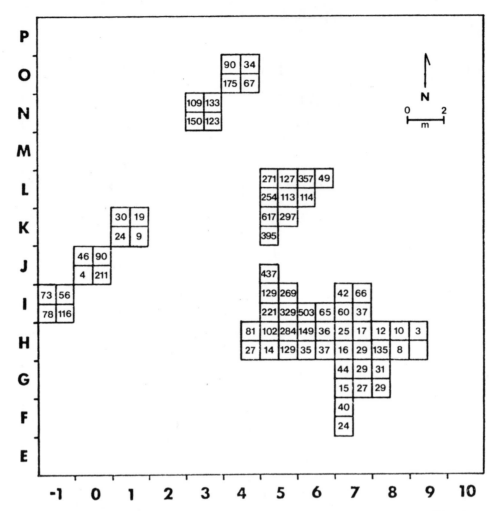

Figure 42. Horizontal distribution of flake debris, with the frequencies per unit plotted, all levels combined.

Some levels must be combined to obtain sufficient sample sizes to graphically compare the horizontal distributions through the vertical column. The mode, or portion of the distribution containing most of the specimens, occurs at a depth of between 10–25 cm (Figure 40), leaving the 0–10 cm and 25+ cm groups corresponding to the tails of the distribution. These divisions are used to compare visually the vertical distributions of flake debris and microblades. In this case biface thinning flakes are not separated from the flake debris because their small number creates a very sparse distribution.

For each vertical interval (Figure 43), the density (artifact-per-unit) threshold used to portray concentrations was deliberately varied to enhance the horizontal patterning and achieve a balance between those units having few specimens (for which a relatively high threshold would yield no visual discrimination), and those units having many specimens (for which a relatively low threshold would result in a confusing mass of contour lines). The

exercise results in limited visual patterning, partly as a result of the noncontiguous array of excavation units that leave many gaps in the grid. Below 25 cm the high artifact densities form two groups in the central portion of the site, for both flake debris and microblades. That general grouping is continued in the 10–25 cm level, with two small outlying pockets (Units N3 and H8) added to the flake debris distribution. The least concordance occurs in the 0–10 cm level, in which the microblade concentration shrinks to two central units and the flake debris keeps its two central concentrations while expanding to an outlying pocket (Units N3 and O4), losing a second one (Unit H8), and adding another (Unit I1).

It is not possible to exclude most explanations for this variability in distribution. Some shifts and omissions in the artifact distribution are so marked that field cataloging error is suspected. This would explain, for example, situations in which a 5 cm level in a unit contains no flake debris, but the levels above and below contain many specimens, as do the same 5 cm levels of the eight surrounding units. The interpretive effects of this error are lessened but not eliminated by the prior combination of several vertical levels for comparative purposes, using the modal 10–25 cm increment.

Statistical procedures might complement the visual exercise, but small sample sizes for individual units—especially in the 0–10 cm and 25+ cm levels—inhibit their use. However, if depth is ignored, the sample sizes are increased sufficiently to show simply the horizontal correlation between flake debris and microblade distribution (Figure 44). Two concentrations of flake debris occur in the central portion of the site, with an outlier in Unit I1, and the same pattern is repeated by the distribution of microblades. Given the lack of excavation units between the two concentrations, they could be manifestations of one larger concentration (which was likely removed by the excavations in the 1930s). This covariation supports an association between the microblade assemblage and the core-flake assemblage.

SUMMARY OF DATING EFFORTS, RESULTS, AND INTERPRETATION

Until now, the dating of the Campus Site has been based almost solely on typological comparisons between certain artifacts—especially those resulting from microblade technology—and similar assemblages from dated sites (West 1975). It is useful to set aside temporarily any presupposed chronological implications of the artifacts themselves, and examine the dating issue independent of typological comparisons. In this way it may be possible to use the site to date the assemblage, rather than use the assemblage to date the site. Three primary questions are:
1. To what extent has the deposit suffered vertical mixing?
2. How many separate occupations are represented at the site?
3. What are their dates?

The deposit has likely undergone some vertical mixing, since cryoturbation is assumed simply by virtue of the site's location and proximity to locales with definite ice wedges, but mixing is also indicated by the presence of a few historic trash items down to depths of 35 cm, and by the occurrence of two charcoal samples of recent origin below 20 cm. However, the majority of the radiocarbon dates are in proper stratigraphic order, suggesting some vertical integrity to the deposit. It would seem fair to say that there has been some mixing, but that the deposit is not completely mixed.

In evaluating the number of separate occupations at the site, the most telling evidence is the vertical and horizontal distribution of artifacts (Figures 40, 43, 44). The vertical distributions of microblades, flakes, and biface

thinning flakes are each unimodal, and the modes of each artifact class coincide—at a depth of 10–15 cm. Generally, from (combined) level to level, microblades and flakes are found in similar horizontal patterns, implying a relatively restricted depositional event for the majority of artifacts. A necessary assumption is that successive occupations of the site through millennia would not have used identical ratios of microblade, biface, and core/flake technologies in their lithic tradition.

On the other hand, the radiocarbon assays indicate at least two different periods of burning at the site (excluding the demonstrably modern burning)—once between 3,500 - 2,725 B.P., and again at 650 B.P. The older period is represented by three dates obtained from three separate areas of the site, while a single sample yielded the 650 B.P. date. If all four samples are accepted as cultural in origin, then the dates suggest that the majority of the cultural activity at the site took place between 3,500 - 2,725 B.P., with less extensive activity at about 650 B.P. If the more recent radiocarbon date is accepted as a valid indicator of cultural activity at the Campus Site, then the radiocarbon dates suggest two phases of activity, albeit one more extensive than the other, while the artifact distribution suggests only one occupation.

Any association between the radiocarbon dates and the artifacts must be inferred indirectly, as no features of any kind were available to date directly. The conclusion made here is that the most extensively distributed suite of radiocarbon dates—from 3,500 - 2,725 B.P.—originated from the same cultural activity responsible for the majority of the artifacts. That is, the majority of the radiocarbon dates are associated with the majority of the artifacts, so that the bulk of the collection—including the microblade material—would be attributable to the 3,500 - 2,725 B.P. range. This raises the question of which, if any, artifacts can be attributed to the 650 B.P. activity, since the vertical distribution of artifacts is unimodal and implies only one period of activity. There is little basis for selecting out certain artifact classes and attributing them to the later 650 B.P. activity, although West (1967:371) suggests that the notched points derive from activity later than that responsible for the microblade material. A case might be made for the groundstone artifact being of later origin, since elsewhere such artifacts occur in contexts indicating Athabascan affinities (Rainey 1940:368, Shinkwin 1979:133). One can hardly dispute the idea that the Campus Site locality, given its topographical situation, may have attracted people more than once.

But the existing Campus Site data affords little opportunity to attribute particular artifacts or artifact classes to any but one major activity phase—between 3,500 - 2,725 B.P. Although perhaps not as likely, other possibilities cannot be completely eliminated, such as the earlier or later dates perhaps originating from a forest fire. If the

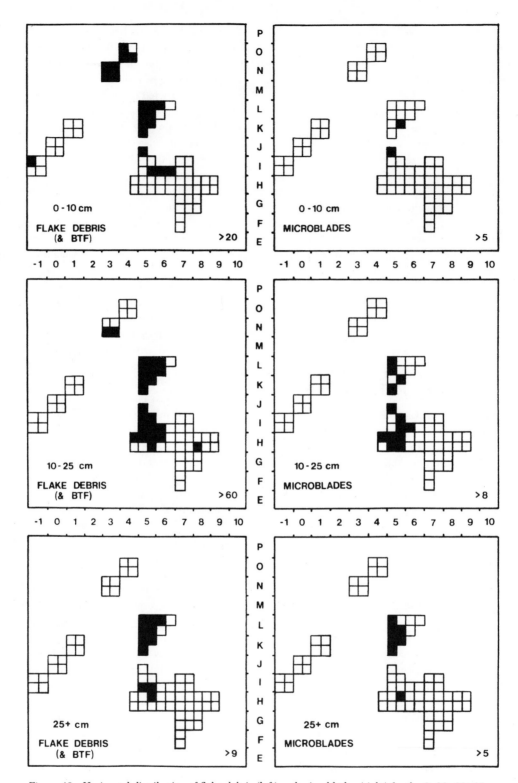

Figure 43. Horizontal distribution of flake debris (left) and microblades (right) for the 0–10, 10–25, and 25+ cm levels. Density threshold for each grid is given at the lower right.

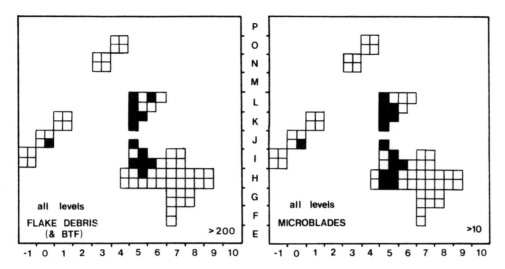

Figure 44. Horizontal distribution of flake debris (left) and microblades (right), all levels combined. Density threshold is given at the lower right.

older dates were of natural origin, for example, then all the artifacts might reflect aboriginal activity dating to 650 B.P. But again, this is considered unlikely. It is significant that the search for datable charcoal and bone samples, with broad horizontal and vertical representation, turned up no assays older than 3,500 B.P. To conclude, the Campus Site restudy has acquired new data concerning the temporal affiliations of the site, but it has not completely eliminated the chronological ambiguity which has plagued it. It does appear that the site is much more recent than the estimated 12,000 to 8,000 B.P. range proposed by West (1975). It is probable that the majority of the artifacts, including the microblade material and other artifact classes represented by more than a few specimens (such as the lanceolate points), date from 3,500 to 2,725 B.P.

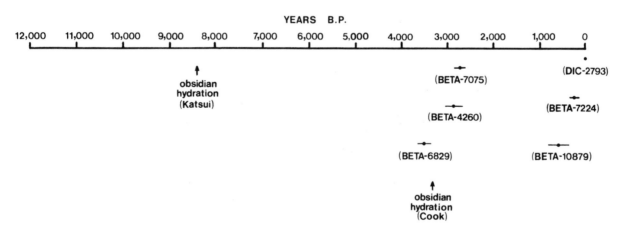

Figure 45. Radiocarbon and obsidian hydration dates plotted on time scale. Standard deviations for radiocarbon dates are indicated by lines equidistant from the dot.

Site Activities

The stone artifacts and fauna collected from the Campus Site give some insight into the lives of the prehistoric people that camped there. Since the excavations of the 1930s, researchers have made brief suggestions about the range of activities practiced there. Archaeological data is never complete enough to infer all the events in a given place and time, but the artifact analysis does allow some discussion about the tasks taking place at the Campus Site in prehistory.

Stone Tool Manufacture and Raw Material Procurement

That tool manufacture took place at the Campus Site is unambiguously indicated by the lithic debris, confirming that microblade production, biface reduction, burination, and core/flake reduction were practiced on-site. There is no indication that macroblade production occurred on-site, since macroblade cores are lacking, and fully half of the macroblades are retouched into tools—which are more likely to be kept on the person and transported from place to place. Lithic debris resulting from retouching stone tools is not sufficiently diagnostic to be discriminated in the assemblage, but it is probable that tools were retouched at the Campus Site.

Some comments can be made about the raw materials obtained for making stone tools. Chert cobbles are found in the Tanana River (Cook 1969:73–74), although the exact places where they were available when the Campus site was occupied is not known. The Chena River has a smaller watershed than the Tanana River, but it is closer (less than two km distant from the Campus Site), and probably has a range of flakable materials similar to that exposed by the Tanana because both rivers cut across similar outwash deposits. The six unaltered cobbles in the collection indicate that on occasion, the raw material was brought directly to the site and used to begin tool manufacture. About 1.7% of the chert flakes contain some cortex on their dorsal surface, and 1.4% of the complete flakes and proximal flake fragments have cortex platforms. When the total chert artifact inventory is inspected, closer to 2.5% of the sample displays some cortex. This increase is in part a reflection of the larger size of formal tools, which increases the probability that they will retain cortical portions of the original cobble.

However, if *initial* flaking, in any of the represented lithic technologies, was conducted at the site, then a higher proportion of unaltered cobbles, NDS, and cortical

flakes would be expected. The low frequencies of such artifacts suggest that at another location—perhaps the river bed or other gravel source—chert cobbles were tested for flaking characteristics and reduced into rough form. The lack of bifaces classifiable as rough-outs is further support for initial chert cobble reduction taking place elsewhere. In interior Alaska, initial lithic reduction at locations other than that represented by the archaeological assemblage has been inferred from low percentages of decortication flakes: 2% at the Landmark Gap Trail Site (Mobley 1982:97), 6% at the Carlo Creek Site (Bowers 1980:108–119), and 5.3% and 7.1% at sites near Lake Minchumina (Holmes 1986:134).

Sample sizes are much lower for the artifacts of quartz and the two coarse raw materials, but their characteristics are much the same as that for chert. Cores of those materials are rare, as are decortication flakes and unaltered cobbles. The quartz collection includes an unusually high frequency of NDS (seven, or 39% of the 18 debris specimens), probably partly as a function of the flaws common to the material (Crabtree 1967b:11), and partly due to the difficulty in differentiating shattered cleavage planes from flake scars on quartz. Also, quartz outcrops and cobbles can be found about five km to the north of the site in the Goldstream Valley, so differential accessibility may have been a factor in the manipulation of quartz.

Obsidian, which constitutes 2.3% of the total artifact collection, is not locally available in the Fairbanks area. Geological occurrences in Alaska are known from such places as the Aleutian Islands (McCartney 1977:108–109), the Talkeetna Mountains in south-central Alaska (Orth 1967:371), and along the Taylor Highway in east-central Alaska and at Mt. Drum in the Copper River Basin (Cook 1969:75). Other, unconfirmed sources are thought to be present near Mount McKinley, Lake Clark, and elsewhere. The Batza Tena obsidian localities, in the Koyukuk River drainage, seem to have been a preferred source in prehistory and have been well documented in several studies (Patton and Miller 1970; Clark 1972, 1984a).

Artifacts of obsidian from the Campus Site and other Alaskan sites have been analyzed using neutron activation by John P. Cook, who evaluated geological origin and hydration rind thickness. Data on five samples, made available by Cook (personal communication), indicate that three specimens definitely match the Batza Tena Group B or Group B′ composition, while two others are from a related but distinctly different flow. Hydration measurements (conducted by Cook for dating purposes) of the

Campus Site specimens have a wide range, from 0.73 to 3.09 microns, comparable to those found in archaeological specimens from sites at Lake Minchumina (Holmes 1986:131). It can be concluded that the occupants of the Campus Site used obsidian procured from the Batza Tena source, 250 km to the northwest, as well as one other Batza Tena locality (Cook, personal communication).

Macroscopically there is some variability in the obsidian from the Campus Site. Some specimens are extremely black and opaque; others are quite translucent. Several specimens have a distinctive brown tinge, and others contain parallel opaque bands spaced quite closely together. Since there can be macroscopic variability in a single obsidian flow, caution must be exercised in suggesting that these materials are from different geological sources. All are within the range of variability of the Batza Tena sources (Cook, personal communication).

In the obsidian debris assemblage (including NDS and biface thinning flakes), 4.7% (nine out of 193 specimens) displayed cortex on their dorsal surfaces. About 5.4% of the complete and proximal obsidian flakes were struck from cortex platforms. This is approximately three and four times the frequency of cortical elements as compared to the chert debris assemblage, and the obsidian tools show a tendency to have cortical surfaces also. This is so despite the much greater distance to the obsidian source, suggesting that unaltered Batza Tena obsidian cobbles could be relied upon to have excellent flaking qualities without experimental test fracturing at the source, and the smooth, rounded original cobble was an acceptable form for long distance transport (Holmes 1986:134–135).

Other Maintenance Activities

The relative importance of stone tool manufacture, as opposed to other maintenance activities, can be assessed in one way by comparing the amount of lithic debris to the numbers of complete and broken tools, using the total 1960s (controlled recovery) assemblage. Flakes, NDS, and biface thinning flakes constitute 88.8% of the controlled collection. The relative numbers of tools are an indication that other activities besides stone tool manufacture were important at the Campus Site. Without conduct-

ing functional analyses on the stone tools, those exact activities can only be hinted at; this study has avoided the use of functional artifact terms such as "knives" and "scrapers." Nonetheless, it is likely that some of the bifaces, retouched specimens, and flakes served cutting and scraping functions.

Charcoal and bone specimens attest to people using fire and eating at the Campus Site. Certainly fires were used for both heat and cooking, although the charcoal was scattered through the site matrix, rather than being concentrated in discrete areas or hearths. There is no firm evidence of structures or other features.

The bone sample, although small, documents use of some local fauna, summarized in the fauna chapter. Large and small game are represented. Many of the bones were crushed into small pieces and cooked or burned at the site, characteristic of the method for making "bone grease" (Leechman 1951).

The Campus Site may have served as a base camp from which hunting forays were made, as its location on the rim of a bluff provides good visibility to the east and south. Projectile points in the collection document the possession of weapons. Looking out over the Chena and Tanana River floodplains, animals and people would have been most visible in the winter when deciduous foliage is gone. Alternatively, the location may have been selected for its defensive qualities, as approach is moderately difficult up the bluff from the east and south. Whether for hunting or defense, it seems apparent that the site was situated to take advantage of the view. The relatively flat terrain just 100 meters further up from the bluff was apparently disdained in favor of occupying the more steeply sloped brow of the hill. There are in the collections of the University of Alaska Museum, however, several isolated bifaces with provenience designations indicating discovery elsewhere on the college campus.

The Campus site was originally termed a "camp site" by Rainey (1939), in reference to the lack of housepits and other structural features. Fifty years later that characterization seems still appropriate. The range of site activities indicated by the artifact assemblage suggests no more than the normal tasks expected for a temporary occupation.

A REVIEW OF THE CAMPUS SITE IN LIGHT OF NEW DATA

The intent of the Campus Site restudy project was to compile all information about the site and its collections into one comprehensive volume. An emphasis has been placed on artifact description, since the artifact collections have been the main source of inference about the site. Moreover, discussion about the technological processes of artifact manufacture has been included in the belief that "end products alone . . . are not sound individual indicators of a prehistoric culture or prehistoric cultural change because of the various morphological changes they undergo while in a systemic context as a result of skill or lack of skill, breakage and rejuvenation, hafting, and use" (Flenniken 1984:199). The study has been primarily inductive, and the intent has been to maintain a standard of objectivity allowing other researchers to use the information to support their own various hypotheses and models of human behavior. Yet some summary generalizations about the results of the study are in order.

Descriptions of the Campus Site and its artifacts have been made by other researchers: this restudy project differs from previous analyses in that more of the complete excavated sample was available. Thus a more thorough characterization of the artifact assemblage—including metric and discrete attributes of various artifact types—can now be based on the increased sample. The faunal material identified by Lobdell and presented in this volume was heretofore unreported. And finally, the restudy project has produced new information concerning the age of the Campus Site and its collections. Thus this concluding chapter compares the current results with previous characterizations of the Campus Site material: it does not focus upon intersite comparisons with North American or Old World sites.

Assemblage Characteristics

Lists of artifact types present at the Campus Site were compiled by Nelson (1937:267–272) and Rainey (1939:383), but the meanings then assigned to some of those names have changed with time. Classificatory terms used by Hosley and Mauger (1967:6–9), West (1967:372), and others are not obsolete, but they incorporate functional designations unconfirmed by use-wear analysis or other independent corroboration on the Cam-

pus Site specimens. Consequently the artifact typology used in this restudy project, attempting to discuss the assemblage from a morphological and technological perspective, diverges somewhat from previous inventories (Table 5). Descriptive detail presented in this analysis should allow researchers to correlate artifact classes so affected, such as the traditional "end scraper," which in this analysis would be termed a flake with short axis retouch.

In this restudy the chipped stone artifacts have been discussed as the result of a series of technological systems and sub-systems: microblade technology, macroblade technology, biface technology, core/flake technology, retouching, and burination. Miscellaneous stone artifacts are attributed to hammering and grinding activities. The discussion considers both the process and the product of these technologies (as well as the raw materials used), and compares them with previous characterizations of the Campus Site.

RAW MATERIAL CHARACTERIZATIONS

Terms used by early researchers for the types of stone worked by the Campus Site craftsmen included "quartz, quartzite, basanite, chert, jasper, obsidian, and moss agate" (Nelson 1937:268, Rainey 1939:384). Hosley and Mauger (1967:6) comment that "striking is the range of color and quality of raw material, mostly varieties of chert." The five raw material categories discriminated in the present analysis—obsidian, quartz, chert, coarse material with conchoidal fracture, and coarse material with tabular fracture—lumped together stone with macroscopically obvious color and quality variability. This increased sample sizes for the material groups, and was suitable for the technological generalizations desired from the artifact analysis. No previous study has attempted to quantify the artifacts in terms of their raw material.

PROCESS OF MICROBLADE TECHNOLOGY

The microblade technology began with selection of a suitable chert cobble. Rarely the cobble was simply split and the fresh facet used as a platform to produce microblades. More often a flake or biface was first manufactured to serve as the core from which microblades were to be removed. Unifacial and bifacial retouch was used to create a straight ridge on the intended blade face, to direct the first spall removal. The platform was sometimes prepared through removal of a single large spall that created one large facet, but more often steep unifacial or bifacial retouch was used to form the platform. Microblade removal was accomplished unidirectionally, with no core rotation. Most often rejuvenation of the core platform was done using a single force executed head-one toward the blade face: less often the force was applied from other angles. One deliberate method of rejuvenation used sequential forces applied perpendicular to the long axis of the core, each oriented so that the bulb of force of the rejuvenation flake was aligned directly below the concavity left from the previous rejuvenation flake removal (resulting in distinctive rejuvenation flakes termed "gull-wing" flakes). When no longer serviceable, microblade cores were discarded with no apparent attempt at secondary use as tools.

The first and for a long time the only description of the microblade manufacturing process at the Campus Site was that of Nelson (1937:270–272), who likened them to examples from the late Neolithic of France:

> . . . cores are in most cases not derived directly from complete nodules but from nondescript spalls perhaps already provided with a thick flat edge serviceable as a striking platform without much preparation. . . . a transverse spall from one of the rounded ends . . . yielded the flat surface intended to serve as a striking platform. . . . the body . . . was flaked transversely all over on both faces, the result being a long, roughly celt- or tongue-shaped affair with two (sometimes three) thin lateral margins. . . . the cross-section of the fully prepared core was usually double convex. The final step was the removal of the desired longitudinal flakes, which was done presumably by indirect blows delivered near the edge of the striking platform, the first flakes to be removed being those embodying the thin lateral core margins where the least resistance was offered. . . . flakes were by degrees removed from all around the block. . . . the Fairbanks cores are comparatively crude, none having reached the final or conical stage.

This early description of microblade manufacture at the Campus Site is largely accurate. Nelson acknowledged exceptions to the prevalent use of flakes or bifaces as the blank for core preparation, so that description (in this volume) of the cortical cobble (Specimen #67–4798) used for microblade production simply confirms his assertion. But platform preparation of the cores is now seen as more complex than he recognized over fifty years ago, and re-

searchers today would not characterize the specimens as "crude" nor assume that a conical form was the intended "final" stage.

The attention given in this study to inferring the sequence of manufacturing steps for microblade technology is prompted by the hope on the part of some researchers that subtle variability in the options selected by prehistoric craftsmen to produce microblades and microblade cores is temporally or spatially diagnostic (Morlan 1973, Sanger 1970, Hayashi 1968, Irving 1956:63). The sequence of steps suggested by this analysis of the Campus Site does diverge slightly from earlier descriptions, but it is not always possible to determine to what extent some of those descriptions refer strictly to the Campus Site material because they often generalize about a group of sites. This is true of the original four sites (including the Campus Site) grouped and described as the Denali Complex (West 1967), contributing to Hayashi's (1968:176) statement that West's original technological description of the cores is "rather ambiguous."

The manufacturing process described herein, especially the platform preparation and rejuvenation methods, is more complex and variable than implied by Morlan's (1970:33) summary, which stated that "the Campus technique . . . consists of fashioning a blank on either a flake or a biface worked from a flake and then forming a platform by means of a burin blow along one margin of the flake." Hayashi (1968:176) is correct in inferring, from the scars on the cores themselves, that two rejuvenation techniques were used: latitudinal flaking, sometimes producing the "gull-wing" flakes, and longitudinal flaking, producing the spalls often termed "core tablets." He goes on to say that "this pattern of core manufacture is identical with the Towarubetsu phase of the Yubetsu tradition." Speaking of the Denali complex in general and the Campus Site in particular, Morlan (1978:102) states:

> I would also agree that their manufacturing process is very similar to the Yubetsu technique . . . [but] they are even more similar to the flake-based techniques of Hokkaido which succeed the Yubetsu process. The major differences seem to reside in the more delicate treatment of the platforms and the consistently smaller size of the Denali specimens.

However, it is still not yet clear that minute technological distinctions at the level made by Hayashi (1968) are uniformly useful for culture chronological discrimination. The microblade core manufactured from a cobble is aberrant in the context of the remainder of the Campus Site microblade core sample, for example, and would expand the range of "techno-types" identified by Smith (1974) in the collection. Yet Smith (1974:351) implies that useful culture chronological distinctions may best be made on the basis of probabilistic generalizations rather than absolute technological preferences, and qualifies his regional construction of the "Northeast Asian-Northwest American Microblade Tradition (NANAMT)" as follows:

> It appears that NANAMT microblade technology involved all three systems simultaneously. A statistically detectable preference for one or two approaches to microblade manufacture is evident when the temporal and spatial distribution of the tradition is followed. Essentially, however, the tradition always consists of a "complex" of core forms that represent multi-variant systems of microblade manufacture.

PRODUCTS OF MICROBLADE TECHNOLOGY

Of the morphologically differentiated products of microblade technology listed in Table 5, most have been identified previously in the Campus Site collection. Nonetheless, it is useful to compare previous qualitative and quantitative characterizations of the artifact types associated with microblade technology with that of this current analysis. Because the morphology of the products is in large part a function of the manufacturing process, there is overlap with this static description of the products with the previous discussion of the manufacturing process. The artifact forms resulting from microblade production are microblade cores, microblades, initial spalls, trifaced ridged flakes, rejuvenation flakes of two kinds, and gull-wing flakes.

Most of the microblade cores in the Campus Site are small thin unifacially or bifacially flaked pieces of stone displaying a plano-convex or convex-convex cross section. One relatively straight edge, truncated obliquely to the axis of the piece by either steep unifacial retouch or a transverse facet executed similarly to a burin removal, served as a blade removal platform. Another edge, consisting of two or more parallel facets forming a "fluted" appearance as a result of successive microblade removals, intersects one end of this platform at slightly less than a 90 degree angle. The remainder of the piece is formed by a slightly concave, straight, or gently convex edge often termed the "keel" or "wedge element" which "extends from the distal end of the flute element to the distal end of the platform element" (Morlan 1970:19). The exception to this generalization is the rather globular specimen (#67–4798, Figure 11, a), which has the cortical remnants of a rounded cobble surface rather than a wedge element.

Although this analysis used a larger sample size of 42 microblade cores from the Campus Site, the basic qualitative morphological generalizations of Rainey (1939:387), West (1967), and others is essentially affirmed. The exceptional cortical cobble specimen does ex-

pand the range of variability usually mentioned, however. Characterizations such as Morlan's (1970:34), which refers to "the Denali complex which has produced cores made exclusively by the F1 sequence," where the F1 sequence specifically excludes those specimens made on weathered nodules, must necessarily be revised. Similarly, so must Hayashi's (1968:178) comment about the Campus Site to the effect that "In spite of the fact that it includes a considerable number of cores (exceeded in number only by the Anangula assemblage), the collection shows only one core type. . . . Every variation in the cores may be placed in sub-types within the range of a single type."

Quantitative statistics on Campus Site microblade cores have been published. Irving (1953:63) stated the largest of the Campus Site cores to be 15 mm wide, with an average of 9 mm wide for the 28 specimens he analyzed, compared to a maximum width of 17.3 mm and an average width of 9.5 mm in the restudy sample of 42 specimens. The attributes of platform length, chord length, and flute length were published by Morlan (1970:23), while Owen (1988:102) measured core length, core width, fluted face height, platform length, platform width, platform angle, and number of facets. In both cases the sample size was 21, consisting of those examples in the University of Alaska Museum. Given the descriptive terms and context of discussion in these two studies, it would appear that Morlan's attribute of platform length is equivalent to Owen's attribute of core length, chord length is equivalent to platform width, and flute length is equivalent to fluted face height. The equivalent terms used in this current Campus Site analysis for those attributes are core length, chord length, and face heights, respectively. Owen (1988:102) does report measurements for "platform length" of the 21 Campus Site specimens but the range is 14.1 - 32.4 mm, or far narrower than that reported by Morlan (1970:23) for the same sample, so in the absence of complete prosaic or illustrated definitions of how that variable was measured it is assumed here that her more comparable measurement is core length. Morlan (1970:23) provides the statistics of mean, standard deviation, and range, while Owen (1988:102) describes the cores in terms of mean, median, and range (Table 17).

With the same sample of specimens, Owen's (1988) and Morlan's (1970) ranges for what seem to be the same variables differ slightly by several millimeters, as do the mean values. This serves as a comment on the reliability of any one individual's observations, points out the need for precise definitions of measured attributes, and suggests that recording in terms of tenths of a millimeter creates a false impression of precision.

Comparing the total sample with that used by Morlan and Owen, both the minimum and maximum values for each of the three attributes measured in the larger sample

Table 17. Comparison of descriptive statistics (in mm) for Campus Site microblade cores.

	Mean	Median	Range	S.D.
Morlan (1970) N = 21				
Platform Length	23.0	—	10 –44	3.9
Chord Length	9.0	—	4 –15	9.0
Flute Length	22.3	—	16 –29	3.7
Owen (1988) N = 21				
Core Length	25.4	23.9	17.2–45.2	—
Platform Width	9.5	9.9	3.6–12.8	—
Fluted Face Height	20.8	19.4	13.6–27.4	—
Total Sample N = 42				
Core Length	24.1	—	15.0–45.6	6.4
Chord Length	9.4	—	4.0–28.1	3.3
Face Length	20.7	—	12.0–28.1	3.9

are within a few millimeters of those reported in the two earlier studies, with one exception. The maximum chord length of 18.6 mm recorded for the larger sample is a reflection of the core made on a cortical cobble, which has a greater core width and greater chord length. Otherwise measuring the larger sample of 42 specimens, rather than the smaller sample of 21 cores used by Morlan and Owen, does not result in an appreciably different range or mean value for the three attributes. The standard deviation for flute length is similar between the smaller and larger samples, while for core length and chord length it is not, indicating that increasing the size of the sample included more specimens with chord lengths approaching the mean, and included specimens with a core length skewed differently than the smaller sample. In summary, using a larger sample from which to generalize quantitatively about microblade cores at the Campus Site does not appear to produce statistics sufficiently different to cause any changes in inference or interpretation others may have made from previously published data.

Nelson (1937:268) originally described the Campus Site microblades as "small prismatic flakes"—a qualitative characterization that is not substantially altered by this restudy. The width and thickness of nineteen Campus Site microblades was reported by Irving (1953:62), who stated width to range from four to nine mm, with an average of 5.8 mm, and thickness to range from one to 2.5 mm, with an average of 1.7 mm. Quantitative summaries of Campus Site microblades have also been published by Cook (1968) and Owen (1988:85) using samples drawn from the University of Alaska Museum collection. The statistics derived for the two samples are not directly comparable, however, because Cook (1968:121–122) provided a cumulative graph of microblade width and reported coefficients of variation (to contrast samples from several different sites) for the attributes of length, width, and thickness, whereas Owen (1988:85, 354) reported median, mean, range, standard deviation, skewness, and kurtosis for length, width, thickness, and longitudinal thickness. Owen's (1988:279) sample sizes for some attri-

butes vary according to whether the microblade is complete or fragmentary: out of 194 specimens in her sample only six (3%) are complete. For Cook's (1968:122) study 240 microblades were used, but it is not clear how the statistics were adjusted according to whether complete or fragmentary specimens were being measured.

For the Campus Site restudy sample, statistics for length were computed using the sample of 39 complete specimens, while width and thickness statistics were computed using the complete and incomplete samples totaling 604 specimens (Table 7). The same attributes (except for weight, which was not measured) are summarized in Table 18 for Owen's (1988:354) sample. However, direct comparison between Owen's (1988) statistics and those from this restudy or any other sample must be tempered by the facts that: (1) judging from the length range (Table 18), she lumped microblades and macroblades together, and (2) judging from the sample size of 194 (Table 18), compared to her identification of only six complete specimens (Table 19), she included fragments in the analysis of length.

Owen (1988) made other observations on her Campus Site sample, only some of which were repeated on the larger sample in this restudy. A comparison of the "break type" categories (Table 19) shows differences in frequency between the two samples, but probably not sufficient to alter any inferences made from either sample alone. Similarly, comparison of cross-section categorizations for the two samples (realizing that the restudy did not differen-

Table 18. Selected measurements of the blade sample (in mm) reported by Owen (1988:354).

	Length	Width	Thickness
N	194	194	194
Range	3.6–67.7	2.6–20.2	0.7–6.4
Mean	14.99	5.41	1.72
SD	8.05	2.22	0.88
Median	12.75	4.89	1.54
Skewness	2.28	3.50	2.80
Kurtosis	9.63	16.71	10.71

Table 19. Comparison of "break types" for Owen's (1988:279) microblade and macroblade sample and the total restudy microblade sample.

	Complete	Proximal	Medial	Distal
Owen (1988) N = 194	6 (3%)	94 (48%)	58 (30%)	36 (19%)
Total Sample N = 604	39 (6%)	216 (36%)	254 (42%)	95 (16%)

tiate between Owen's (1988:295) categories of two and three-plus dorsal arrises), are not sufficiently different to likely affect substantive generalizations based upon either sample (Table 20). Owen (1988) was attempting to develop an analytical scheme that she could apply uniformly to characterize macroblade and microblade assemblages, and some of her attributes have limited utility for the latter. Available to the specialist in her (1988) volume are statistics for 48 discrete attributes and ten continuous variables.

Not reported previously from the Campus Site was a trifaced ridge flake, to use Kobayashi's (1970:39) term referring to the first spall (resulting from force applied parallel to the axis of the microblade core) that prepared the platform by removing the entire edge from the top of a microblade core blank. The possibility of the technique being occasionally used by the Campus Site stone-workers was left open by Morlan (1978:102), who stated that "their manufacturing process is very similar to the Yubetsu technique," which involves the removal of a trifaced ridge flake from the core to begin initial forming of the platform. Nonetheless, the Campus Site collections contain no "ski-spalls"—long narrow flakes with rectangular cross sections produced by second and third removals following the trifaced ridge flake removal—which characterize the Yubetsu technique (Morlan 1967:177). In regard to northeast Asia analogues, Hayashi (1968:177), however, uses a suite of criteria to suggest alternatively that "the technological attributes of the Campus cores, together with the inventory of the associated implements, indicates that they were rooted in the horizon of proto-Fukui technology."

The nine initial spalls from microblade core preparation found in the Campus Site collection show evidence of both unifacial and bifacial alignment of the ridge used to

Table 20. Comparison of cross-section types for Owen's (1988:295) microblade and macroblade sample and the total restudy microblade sample.

	Triangular	Trapezoidal	>Two Dorsal Arrises
Owen (1988) N = 194	36 (19%)	124 (64%)	34 (18%)
Total Sample N = 604	169 (28%)	---------435 (72%)---------	

guide the spall removal, as noted by Mauger (1971:8). Metric attributes (Table 6) have not been reported elsewhere, as Mauger's (1971) analysis of microblade technology at the Campus Site was essentially qualitative.

Similarly, the 15 "gull-wing flakes", reflecting microblade core rejuvenation using force applied from the side of the core, were heretofore reported from the Campus Site only qualitatively by Mauger (1971:9), although he used the term "side struck platform flakes." The other form of core platform rejuvenation flake, reflecting force applied directly towards the blade face, has also been noted in the Campus Site collections (Cook 1968:124–125, Mauger 1971:19–20, Morlan 1970:33). The platform rejuvenation discussion in this volume is an elaboration, using a larger sample size, upon the process as discussed in earlier studies. The description of core platform rejuvenation generalized by West (1981:122) for assemblages he includes in the Denali Complex is essentially accurate for the Campus Site material, except that the "gull-wing" aspect of the technological system was not recognized.

PROCESS AND PRODUCTS OF MACROBLADE TECHNOLOGY

Although Rainey (1939:384–385) used the term "blade" to refer to artifacts in the Campus Site collection, and illustrated one example (Specimen 4 in his Figure 7; Specimen c in Figure 28 of this volume), the macroblade technology has received little attention in analyses of the Campus Site material. Hosley and Mauger (1967:9) commented that "the importance of these large blades as a significant component of the Campus Site has previously not been recognized," likely because no macroblade cores were recovered. Their description of the specimens as "trapezoidal in cross section, two or three-faceted on the dorsal side, and parallel-sided," is primarily the set of criteria used for discriminating them in the first place: their comment that the few facets on the platforms "implies a high degree of chipping skill rather than extensive core preparation" seems unwarranted (Hosley and Mauger 1967:9).

But in the absence of cores, the macroblade technology can only be partially reconstructed from the twelve recovered specimens. The six complete or proximal specimens show multifaceted platforms and some dorsal reduction and alignment in preparation for blade removal. Six macroblades were subsequently retouched. A medial macroblade fragment snapped in the manner of a historic gunflint was previously unreported from the Campus Site: it may reflect a legitimate prehistoric stone-working technique in interior Alaska. Medial segments of deliberately snapped macroblades are a major element in the artifact inventory on Anangula Island in the Aleutians, for example (Aigner 1970:67); the author has observed in other

Aleutian collections snapped medial macroblade fragments with pronounced bulbs of force on the snap very similar to the Campus Site specimen.

PROCESS AND PRODUCTS OF BIFACE REDUCTION

Little discussion about the process of biface production at the Campus Site has appeared in previous literature, so no comparative discussion is warranted here, and the earlier discussion of the biface reduction process will suffice. But the products of biface reduction, mainly the more symmetrical forms usually assumed to have been finished tools, have received attention in previous literature ever since Nelson (1937:268) reported "biface blanks suitable for knives or spearpoints: knives or spearpoints; [and] arrowpoints respectively with straight base, simple stem, and side notches."

The lanceolate specimens have been the subject of most interest to researchers, in part because of their possible relationships with fluted points, which are associated with early sites in North America (Clark 1984b). MacNeish (1959:7) termed the Campus Site specimens "Agate Basin-like points," and included the site as part of the Northwest Microblade Tradition in his far-ranging evolutionary model of northern North American prehistory. Terms taken from the literature on PaleoIndian occupations in North America were also used by West (1967:374), who stated that one biface from the Campus Site resembled a "Milnesand" point, and by Hosley and Mauger (1967:9–10), who called one specimen a "Lerma-like point," identified two more as "cascade points," and stated that "the general feeling of these is that of the Northern Point or Plano tradition." Similarly, Bandi (1969:50) referred to the Campus Site material as including "a series of projectile points suggestive of Paleo-Indian influences," and Workman (1974:102), in his paper entitled "First Dated Traces of Early Holocene Man in the Southwest Yukon Territory, Canada," compared "finished bifaces with highly convex bases (probable projectile points)" with "one unpublished specimen from 1966 excavations at the Campus site, an undated station of presumed moderate antiquity." Some specimens were referred to by West (1967:372, 374) as "biconvex bi-pointed knives," a functional designation with which Hayashi (1970:173) takes issue. Citing the presence of basal grinding equally on both edges, the latter author considered the specimens to be projectile points, rather than knives. The present analysis also indicates a relatively equal degree of grinding on both edges of such specimens. Furthermore, the number of such specimens is apparently greater than previously thought, because incomplete bifaces once classified as distal point fragments are—by virtue of edge grinding—likely basal fragments of lanceo-

late points. The association of lanceolate projectile point forms with microblade materials elsewhere in the Pacific Northwest has been noted by Sanger (1968b:100), who mentions that "the leaf-shaped points are small, well made, and within the range of Cascade points" as described by Butler (1960).

The presence of two side-notched projectile points in the Campus Site collection has been noted previously by Hosley and Mauger (1967:10–11), who compared them with those of Palisades II and Band 6 at Onion Portage (Anderson 1968). The two points were also noted by West (1981:227), who questioned their cultural association with the microblade material.

Little attention has been given to the assortment of other bifacial artifacts in the Campus Site collection, other than statements to the effect that some existed; Hosley and Mauger (1967:9–10) identified these specimens functionally as knives. West (1981:Table 3.3) includes "lenticular bifaces" for the Campus Site entry in his table of selected artifact types from "Beringian Tradition Assemblages of Eastern Beringia." As is evident from the current analysis, several dozen bifaces in addition to those morphological classifiable as projectile points are present in the Campus Site collection. Inferences to be made from the sample include the suggestion that primary reduction of the specimens occurred elsewhere, because specimens with cortical surfaces and "rough-outs" were rare, as were cortical flakes. Several larger specimens display battered edges, suggestive of use for heavy-duty chopping tasks. An emphasis on the final stages of biface manufacture is suggested by the relatively large number of small, irregularly-shaped bifaces and biface fragments, and the fact that almost five percent of the entire collection is composed of biface thinning flakes—an artifact type previously unreported from the Campus Site.

PROCESS AND PRODUCTS OF CORE/FLAKE TECHNOLOGY

Rainey (1939:384) noted the presence of modified and unmodified flakes in the Campus Site material, but cores from which those flakes might have been struck were not reported. It is realized that biface production and other stone-working technologies create nondiagnostic flakes, but the absence of flake cores is notable in the earlier descriptions of the collections. The excavations in 1966 produced only two flake cores, "the pattern of flake removal being random and without pattern" (Hosley and Mauger 1967:9). The entire flake core sample analyzed by the Campus Site restudy project consisted of only 17 specimens—amounting to 0.2% of the total artifact sample. It is not surprising, therefore, that most researchers have overlooked the presence of a core/flake technology at the Campus Site. Perhaps it was simply assumed to be one of the stone-working methods used there because of its simplicity and the fact that most prehistoric sites in Alaska contain evidence of some form of core/flake tradition. In his original definition of the Denali Complex, which used the Campus Site as one of the four type sites for the complex, West (1967:369) identified the presence of modified flakes, but made no mention of flake cores. Similarly, no attention has been drawn to the presence of nondiagnostic shatter in the lithic material from the Campus Site. Flakes are the single most common artifact class in the Campus Site collection, despite statements to the contrary that microblades are "the most frequently occurring artifact" in the Denali Complex (West 1981:123: repeated in Owen 1988:55).

Thus, the discussion of core/flake technology presented in this study has little parallel in other literature about the Campus Site. To summarize, the scarcity of specimens with cortex (from artifacts reflecting *any* of the lithic technologies identified in the collections), the low number of flake cores, and the low incidence of nondiagnostic shatter indicates that primary reduction took place away from the Campus Site. Furthermore, although chert, obsidian, quartz, and coarse-grained rock are represented in the core assemblage, the flake and tool assemblage contains many other macroscopically distinguishable chert "types." Large flakes were often used subsequently as cores from which other flakes were struck, and core rotation was common.

PRODUCTS OF RETOUCHING

Retouched specimens at the Campus Site were noted in the first papers published, where they were given functional terms such as end scrapers, side scrapers, or retouched blades (Nelson 1935:356, 1937:269; Rainey 1939:384). At the time, they were recognized as having limited diagnostic value, and Nelson (1937:269) commented that "as examples of an implement having nearly world-wide distribution, they are not unique, except perhaps as regards their relatively small size." The excavations in the 1960s provided more material, summarized by Hosley and Mauger (1967:9) with the statement that "the collection of scrapers and knives exhibits a wide variety of forms and sizes, with readily discernible types being simple side and end scrapers, and sub-triangular "skewed" end scraper type, lamellar scrapers on large blades, and ovate forms." West (1967:372) describes three "scraper" forms from the Campus Site as characteristic of the Denali Complex: "flat-topped end scrapers on thick blade-like flakes often bearing graver spurs. . . . large, angular scrapers bifacially worked with steep retouch on two or more edges. . . . [and] small, roughly triangular end scrapers with pyramidal cross section." Retouched microblades and macroblades were noted

in the Campus Site material by Hosley and Mauger (1967: 7–9).

In the present analysis, which did not include functional analysis, the term scraper was avoided in favor of the morphological term of "retouched specimen." The technique of retouching is viewed as a secondary technological process which can be applied to the products of microblade technology, macroblade technology, and the flakes produced by core/flake technology (or other flake-producing lithic reduction strategies). Retouching can be applied to bifaces as well, but it is then difficult to distinguish from intentional biface reduction unless some criteria, such as edge angle, are singled out to define it. In the absence of such analysis no retouching was identified on bifacial specimens. Using morphological rather than functional terms for the Campus Site material does not change the overall perception of the sample. A wide range of shapes and sizes is evident for retouched flakes, although there is obviously some consistency in the desired form (Figures 32, 33). The presence of graver spurs on scrapers (noted by West 1967:372), in the sense commonly used to describe distinctive retouched specimens elsewhere in North America (Mobley 1983:110–111), was not observed in the Campus Site sample. However, a single flake with a sharply retouched point was identified, as was a single flake with a steeply retouched notch (Figure 34, a, b).

Retouched macroblades were first noted in the Campus Site by Hosley and Mauger (1967:8–9), who reported both "end" (distal) and "side" (lateral) retouch, but the number of specimens was not quantified other than to say that the latter were more prevalent. Six of the twelve Campus Site macroblades are retouched—all dorsally, with five showing lateral retouch and one showing distal retouch. The identification of a possible gunflint was not made prior to this restudy.

The dearth of retouched microblades was noted by Hosley and Mauger (1967:7), who counted only eight that were modified either deliberately or through use. Combining samples from the Campus, Otter Falls, and Donnelly Ridge sites, Cook (1968:122–123) observed a low incidence (four percent) of retouch on microblades, even using magnification to observe subtle modification due to use. Owen (1988:14, 299) identified 10 retouched microblades out of a sample of 194 (or five percent of the sample); "scars were classified as retouch when they were regular in shape, height and patterning." She goes on to divide them according to lateral or distal edges (only one specimen showed distal retouch); dorsal or ventral surfaces; step, hinge, or feather terminations; bifacial or unifacial; and completeness—all criteria which may have diagnostic value in a large sample, but are of limited utility in such a small sample (Owen 1988). Of the 604 microblades (including small fragments) analyzed in the Campus Site restudy project, only three were isolated as re-touched specimens (all showing dorsal lateral retouch). These discrepancies between studies reflect the varying criteria and conservatism in identifying retouch on specimens.

PRODUCTS OF BURIN TECHNOLOGY

The perception of burin technology at the Campus Site has changed since Bandi (1963, 1969:50) summarized burin occurrences in Alaska and claimed that at the Campus Site "burins proper are lacking—i.e., there are only some atypical examples of this type of tool." His comment was perhaps based on Irving's (1955:381) contention that "the Campus site burins . . . lack a distinctive specialized form, being made on flakes or fragments the shape of which is fortuitous" (both burins identified as such by Irving were actually made on bifaces). But in the late 1960s, distinctive burin forms were recognized in the Campus Site material. West (1967:371–372) included burin spalls as an "essential element" of the Denali Complex, as well as Donnelly burins, defined as "burins manufactured on small, flat flakes of irregular outline which may show minute marginal retouch on alternate edges and spall facets on several edges," and noted the latter as present in the Campus Site collection. Burins were mentioned in the new collections obtained in 1966 (Hosley 1966:1, Hosley and Mauger 1967:7–8), with the latter paper referring to them as "notched" burins and briefly discussing their manufacture and use.

In a detailed study of Donnelly burins from the Campus Site, Mauger (1970) distinguished them from bifaces that showed burin scars. Excluding the latter from study (which included the two burin specimens identified in the Campus Site by Irving 1955:381), Mauger focused upon inferring the technological process of burin manufacture through morphological analysis, replicative methods, and use-wear analysis, thus going far beyond the morphological description emphasized in this volume. Whereas the description of Donnelly burins in an earlier chapter was patterned after Mauger's (1970) thorough review, conclusions from his use-wear analysis can be summarized as follows. Microscopically discernible crushing and rounding of burin facet edges "indicates that stress during task performance was perpendicular to the facet edges and parallel to the plane of the facet. . . . this implies that the task of these burins was one of scraping" (Mauger 1970:33). He noted that wear occurs where edge angles are between 60 and 90 degrees (the mode being 80 degrees), and compared it with the wear and edge angle found on distally retouched "scrapers." Despite occasional patches of polish on the sides of the Donnelly burins in the Campus Site collection, Mauger (1970:35) stated that "the lack of gross morphological consistency

and the indication that a great deal of leverage was not involved in using these tools suggests that they were not hafted." He thought they may have been used to smooth rounded objects of antler, much as one might use a broken shard of bottle glass to smooth a dowel, and suggested the term "Campus scraper-burins" (which has not entered into general usage) to capture the morphological and functional character of the type (Mauger 1970:49).

Previous researchers had little comment on the other burin forms in the Campus Site collections, except for Irving's (1955:381) discussion of two bifaces with burin facets (Figures 26, a and 36, f). Four bifaces with burin facets are identified in this volume, and the range in size is expanded to include a long slender biface with a very long burin scar extending almost the length of one edge (Figure 36, h). Other forms not previously noted are flakes with burin scars emanating from a simple snap facet that was used as the platform for the removal, and retouched specimens with burin scars (distinguishable from Donnelly burins; see earlier chapter).

Ten burin spalls were counted in the Campus Site collection by using the presence of a rectangular cross-section as a dominant criterion. Previous studies have counted 14 (Hosley and Mauger 1967:8), but Mauger (1970:23–27), who referred to his sample size only as "a number of spalls," provides ample discussion attesting to the difficulty in distinguishing burin spalls from spalls produced through microblade technology. The discovery of a burin spall joining a Donnelly burin in the Campus Site collection (Figure 36, b, c), and observation of other burin spalls in the sample, suggests that burin manufacture may often have involved a snapped edge to direct the spall removal—the burin facet consequently paralleling the snapped facet to form a burin spall of rectangular cross-section.

OTHER LITHIC TECHNOLOGIES

A variety of miscellaneous artifact types at the Campus Site was noted by Rainey (1939:384), and Hosley and Mauger (1967:10). Based on a personal communication from H. Morris Morgan, who was in charge of excavations at the site that year, West (1967:360–361) viewed the newly acquired 1966 material as increasing the sample size "without altering the basic categories of artifact forms," which is true to an extent. Unaltered cobbles and pebbles are present in the collection, some of which may have been culturally introduced to the site, as are cobbles showing definite battering indicative of hammerstone use. The collection contains three cobble spalls, one of which was retouched and battered (West 1967:372 considers "boulder chip scrapers" as "frequent constituents" of the Denali Complex). Other miscellaneous items consist of a flaked and ground siltstone tool fragment (Figure 23, e), a tabular rock with three small pits worn into it by the rotary motion of some pointed object, and a pumice cobble with grooves abraded into it (Figure 23, j).

THERMAL ALTERATION OF LITHIC MATERIALS

It would appear that deliberate thermal alternation of lithic materials, to improve their flaking quality, has not been previously considered by researchers interested in the Campus Site. While indications of thermal alteration were monitored in the restudy, and some specimens showed coloration changes and thermal fractures (2.5% of the debris assemblage, for example), neither the patterns of thermal modification in the collection nor the spatial distribution of those specimens is sufficient to suggest that it was done deliberately by the aboriginal craftsmen. Instead it would seem that the artifacts were heated either accidently by the prehistoric inhabitants, or perhaps by later historic fires (no evidence suggests that natural forest fires were the cause).

Expansion of the Fauna Data

The faunal identifications accomplished by Lobdell for this study form the only comprehensive list ever compiled for the Campus Site (Table 15). Other researchers have simply mentioned the presence of burned and calcined bone (Hosley and Mauger 1967:6). While the inferences to be made from the few bear, beaver, hare, and possibly wolf and bison bones present in the sample are limited, at least the faunal assemblage is no longer an unexplored avenue for additional archaeological inference.

Number of Occupations and Age of the Campus Site

The additions to and revisions of previous perceptions of the Campus Site artifact collections may be modest but welcome contributions of the restudy, but it is the dating of the site which will receive the most scrutiny. The early temporal estimates of Nelson (1935:356, 1937:269) and Rainey (1939:389) were little more than intuitive guesses based on comparisons with Old World Assemblages. West's (1967:379, 1975:78–79, 1981:131–132) controversial Denali Complex is fundamentally based on the idea of an exclusive techno-complex featuring microblade technology in Alaska between 12,000–8,000 B.P. But more recent dates for occurrences of microblade technology at selected sites in Alaska, and the growing number of sites (sometimes with arguable dating contexts) containing both notched points (usually attributed to the later Northern Archaic tradition) and microblade technology in

the region are calling into question the temporal exclusiveness of microblade technology (Dixon 1985:53–61, Holmes 1986:156–158, Cook and McKennan 1970:2–3, Cook and Gillispie 1986, Dumond 1977:40, Powers and Hoffecker 1989:270–285).

Nonetheless, the typological grounds for attributing the Campus Site to an early Holocene time period are compelling for some, particularly when the microblade cores from sites such as Dry Creek near Healy, dated to about 10,500 B.P. (Powers and Hoffecker 1989:270), are so similar to those from the Campus Site. On the other hand, Owen (1988:118) in some cases discussed the Campus Site as a unit together with the Otter Falls site (dated to 4,570 +/− 150, according to Workman 1978:186), because the "microblade collections are so similar in all aspects."

Preliminary data on radiocarbon dating efforts for the Campus Site (Mobley 1983b, 1984, 1985) were welcomed by regional prehistorians, some of whom used them to support the idea of a late microblade tradition in Alaska (Dixon 1985:49, Holmes 1986:139, Owen 1988:275). Prior to this study, no radiocarbon dates were available from the site. No assayed Campus Site materials were found to date older than 3,500 +/− 140 B.P.: two other samples were found to date to 2,860 +/− 180 and 2,725 +/− 125 B.P. The unimodal vertical distributions of microblades, flakes, and biface thinning flakes (Figure 40) is interpreted as supporting the temporal association of microblade, core/flake, and biface reduction technologies at the site. Similarly, the horizontal distribution of microblades and flakes is similar throughout the site (Figures 41, 42, 43), which is taken to further support that association of the technologies. As stated elsewhere in this volume, the data is interpreted as reflecting occupation much more recent that the time range attributed to the Denali Complex (12,000–8,000 B.P.), and it is probable that most of the artifacts date to between approximately 3,500–2,725 B.P. It is proposed that the Campus Site reflects occupation by a group of people relatively discrete in time (3,500–2,725 B. P.), with possibly some minor activity in later prehistory.

Despite the radiocarbon dates and spatial data from the Campus Site, there will very likely continue to be those specialists who will rely on selected typological criteria to suggest that at least the microblade material is older than the dates would suggest. For example, the presence of two side-notched points at the Campus Site, which in Alaska are usually found in archaeological contexts more in accord with the radiocarbon dates, has been discounted by West (1967:371, 1981:227):

> The Campus site, despite the occurrence there of two notched points, simply seems too overwhelming Beringian (and specifically Denali culture). . . .

and the notched points there are probably simply intrusive. The characteristically shallow soils of the north, together with shallowly rooted vegetation and the accompanying possibilities of undeterminable previous cycles of denudation and revegetation, render the possibility of intrusion an especially pressing problem there.

Hosley and Mauger (1967:11) also referred to the Campus Site as a multiple component site, but used the phrase to mean multiple technologies were represented in the collection: they go on to propose that "the site may constitute either a unit, reflecting deposition of artifact material by one culture with slight time depth, or deposition by different cultures, or different aspects of the same culture, over a more extensive chronological period."

A Final Comment

The Campus Site was declared by Hayashi (1969:172), upon analysis of the University of Alaska Museum Campus Site collection, to be "one of the most significant bodies of evidence so far reported from Alaska." Yet the Campus Site restudy clearly is not able to answer conclusively all questions regarding the possibility of multiple occupations or dating of the site. In a short paper, Bandi and West (n.d.:14) refer to the Campus Site as a key to solving certain puzzling aspects of Alaskan prehistory, saying that "it is our task to open the lock, definitively, by using it." In the same way, this restudy of the Campus Site is offered not as a conclusive statement about interior Alaskan prehistory, but as a tool for comparing sites and their assemblages and furthering our understanding of past Arctic and subarctic cultures.

Glossary of Terms

ARCHAEOLOGY. The science of interpreting past human behavior from the types and locations of artifacts and features found in archaeological sites.

ARRIS. A ridge formed where two flake scars meet.

ARTIFACT. An object purposefully modified by humans.

ASSEMBLAGE. A collection of specimens with integrity of provenience and thought to reflect a discrete cultural group of the past.

B.P. Before present, meaning the number of years before 1950 A.D.

BASAL. A term referring to the base, or proximal end, of a bifacial point, inferred to be the end affixed to a haft of some other material.

BATTERED. A term describing a stone surface or edge displaying many superimposed small flake scars and impact marks with crushed and abraded arrises, resulting from the application of heavy force.

BIFACE. A piece of stone flaked across two roughly parallel surfaces, using a common edge as the point from which most flakes are removed.

BIFACE THINNING FLAKE. A distinctive spall removed from a biface, displaying a multifaceted flake platform, acute platform-to-dorsal surface angle, and a pronounced lip on the ventral surface just above the bulb of percussion.

BULB. A swelling on the ventral surface of a spall, emanating from the platform, resulting from the shock wave produced through the parent piece of stone at the point of force. When the ventral side of an artifact is not illustrated, convention dictates that a barred arrow be drawn to indicate the location of the bulb on the ventral surface.

BURIN. A spall or more extensively flaked piece of stone with an edge removed through force applied parallel to that edge, leaving a blunted edge formed by a long narrow burin scar.

BURIN SPALL. The thin piece of stone representing the former edge removed from an artifact to form a burin, having either a triangular or rectangular cross section.

CHERT. A sedimentary siliceous stone whose homogeneous texture provides good flaking properties for stone tool manufacture.

COBBLE. A piece of rock about the size of one's fist or smaller, usually rounded due to abrasion from such sources as stream or glacial movement, often showing a weathered rind on its surface called cortex.

CORE. A parent piece of stone from which spalls have been removed.

CORTEX. The weathered rind forming on the outside of a piece of rock that has been exposed to the elements over time.

DEBRIS. Term sometimes used generally to refer to flakes and nondiagnostic shatter thought to be discarded within an archaeological site.

DISTAL. A term describing the end of a spall which is opposite that having the platform and bulb of force; on a bifacial point, the term refers to the pointed end opposite the basal end.

DONNELLY BURIN. A term used to describe burins which have one or more retouched notches to form platforms from which to force off burin spalls.

DORSAL. A term describing the side of the spall which shows the negative flake scars from prior spall removals directed at the parent piece of stone.

FACET. A surface, usually meaning all or a portion of a single negative flake scar.

FLAKE. A spall, having no geometric symmetry, struck from a parent piece of stone.

HOLOCENE. That period since the last glacial ice age; the last 12,000 years.

GULL-WING FLAKE. A distinctive spall resulting from microblade platform preparation, in which force is applied to the platform from the side of the core, taking care to align the point of force directly beneath the negative bulb left by a former spall removal to create a "flying V" profile for the flake.

HAMMERSTONE. A functional term applied to stone objects, often cobbles, showing battered surfaces from which use as a percussion tool is inferred.

HINGE FRACTURE. The termination of a flake or blade detachment which results when the force abruptly turns out toward the surface of the parent piece of material.

INITIAL SPALL. The first microblade (or macroblade) removed from a blade core, characterized by a bifacially or unifacially retouched dorsal ridge down its length.

LANCEOLATE. A term used to describe bifacial points having a symmetrical, narrow, leaf-shaped profile.

LOESS. Fine-grained sediments formed by wind-blown glacial silt.

MACROBLADE. A large narrow piece of stone having a cross section of triangular, trapezoidal, or other prismatic shape, struck purposefully from a macroblade core.

MEDIAL. A term describing the mid-section fragment of a spall or bifacial point.

MICROBLADE. A small narrow sliver of stone having a cross section of triangular, trapezoidal, or other prismatic shape, struck purposefully from a microblade core.

MICROBLADE CORE. The parent piece of stone from which microblades have been removed; specimens of the "Campus Site" type are small thin unifacially or bifacially flaked pieces with one edge specifically modified to serve as a platform to facilitate the removal of microblades, whose removal leaves a set of narrow parallel negative flake scars abruptly adjoining one end of the platform at less than a 90 degree angle (Figure 46).

NEGATIVE SCAR. A facet showing all or a portion of the flake scar on the parent piece, and (if the proximal part of the scar is evident) displaying a concavity from the bulb of force.

NONDIAGNOSTIC SHATTER. Irregular pieces of flakable stone displaying noncortical facets but no complete flake scars, often considered to be the result of inadvertent disintegration of prospective cores during experimentation.

OBSIDIAN. A dark colored—often black—volcanic glass, whose homogeneous texture provides good flaking qualities for stone tool manufacture.

OBSIDIAN HYDRATION DATING. Process of dating obsidian artifacts by measuring the thickness of the hydration "rind"—the depth to which water has penetrated the flaked surface of the artifact—and computing a date based on an estimated rate of water absorption.

PERCUSSION. A means of flaking in which the force is transmitted through sudden impact between two objects.

PLATFORM. A surface—either flaked or cortical—bearing the point of force for removal of a spall from a parent piece of rock.

POSITIVE SCAR. A facet showing all or a portion of the flake scar on the ventral surface of a spall, and (if the proximal part of the scar is evident) displaying a convexity reflecting the bulb of force.

POTLID. A piece of stone popped or cracked off from a parent piece through thermal processes (heating or cooling), characterized by one flat side opposed by a convex, rough-textured side.

PRESSURE. A means of flaking in which the force is transmitted through gradual buildup of pressure between two objects already in contact with one another.

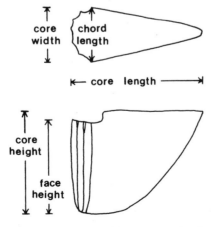

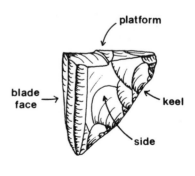

Figure 46. Diagram of the terms used to describe microblade cores.

PROVENIENCE. Location, referring to the horizontal and vertical measurements made on artifacts in place within an archaeological site, and used to make inferences about the meaning of the artifacts and their relationships with one another.

PROXIMAL. A term describing the end of a spall displaying the platform and bulb of force.

RADIOCARBON DATING. A means of determining the age of organic items (that are no older than 50,000 years) by measuring the amount of carbon 14 (a mildly radioactive material) that has decayed into carbon 12 (an inert material) at a fixed rate.

REJUVENATION FLAKE. A spall from a microblade core that removes the prior blade removal platform, usually using force directed parallel to the axis of the platform and head-on at the microblade blade face, often resulting in a spall with a multifaceted platform reflecting the aligned proximal negative flake scars of prior microblade removals.

RETOUCH. The process by which the edges of stone artifacts are modified through the removal of small, overlapping flakes.

SCRAPER. Functional term used by some researchers to describe a stone tool with retouched edges.

SITE. The location of past human activity, reflected physically by artifacts and features.

SPALL. A piece of stone—including microblades, macroblades, and flakes—removed from another using deliberate force.

STEP FRACTURE. The termination of a flake or blade detachment that results when the spall shatters at the distal end, resulting in an abrupt truncation.

STRATIGRAPHY. Term referring to the layers of soil or other materials in archaeological sites or geological contexts.

TRIFACED RIDGE FLAKE. A spall resulting from initial preparation of a microblade core platform, in which the planned core platform is first retouched and then truncated with a burin force, creating a long thin spall that differs from the initial spall of microblade manufacture only in that the tri-faced ridged flake is significantly larger.

UNIFACE. A piece of stone flaked on only one (almost always the dorsal) side, leaving the ventral side unmodified.

VENTRAL. A term describing the side of the spall reflecting the shock wave that sheared it from the parent specimen; consequently the side which would display the bulb of force, if the specimen is complete.

Bibliography

Aamodt, M. W., W. K. Hao, and K. Humphreys. 1968. New diggings from the university slag heap. *Denali: The University of Alaska Yearbook*, 24–29.

Ackerman, R. E. 1980. Microblades and prehistory: Technological and cultural considerations for the north Pacific coast. *Early Native Americans: Prehistoric Demography, Economy, and Technology*, edited by D. L. Browman, 189–197. The Hague: Mouton Publishers.

Addington, L. R. 1986. *Lithic illustration: Drawing flaked stone artifacts for publication*. Chicago: University of Chicago Press.

Aigner, J. S. 1970. The unifacial core and blade site on Anangula Island, Aleutians. *Arctic Anthropology*. 7(2):59–88.

———. 1986. Footprints on the land. *Interior Alaska: A Journey Through Time*, 97–146. Anchorage: Alaska Geographical Society.

Aigner, J. S., and B. Fullem. 1976. Cultural implications of core distribution and use patterns at Anangula, 8500–8000 B.P. *Arctic Anthropology*. 13:(2):71–82.

Alaska Department of Fish and Game. 1973. *Alaska's Wildlife and Habitat: Volume I*. Alaska Department of Fish and Game.

Alaska Department of Fish and Game. 1978a. *Alaska's Wildlife and Habitat: Volume II*. Alaska Department of Fish and Game.

Alaska Department of Fish and Game. 1978b. *Alaska's Fisheries Atlas: Volume I*. Alaska Department of Fish and Game.

Alaska Department of Fish and Game. 1978c. *Alaska's Fisheries Atlas: Volume II*. Alaska Department of Fish and Game.

Anderson, D. D. 1968. A stone age campsite at the gateway to America. *Scientific American*. 218(6):24–33.

———. 1970. Microblade traditions in northwestern Alaska. *Arctic Anthropology*. 7(2):2–16.

Bandi, H. 1963. The burins in the eskimo area. Early Man in the Western Arctic. Ed. by F. H. West. *Anthropological Papers of the University of Alaska*. 10(2):19–28.

———. 1969. *Eskimo Prehistory*. College: University of Alaska Press.

Bandi, H., and F. H. West. n.d. The Campus site and the problem of Epi-Gravettian infiltrations from Asia to America. Manuscript in the possession of the author.

Barton, R. N. E., and C. A. Bergman. 1982. Hunters at Hengistbury: Some evidence from experimental archaeology. *World Archaeology*. 14(2):237–248.

Befu, H., and C. S. Chard. 1960. Preceramic cultures in Japan. *American Antiquity*. 62:815–849.

Bergman, C. A., and M. H. Newcomer. 1983. Flint arrowhead breakage: Examples from Ksar Akil, Lebanon. *Journal of Field Archaeology*. 10:238–243.

Binford, L. R., and G. I. Quimby. 1963. Indian sites and chipped stone materials in the northern Lake Michigan area. *Fieldiana Anthropology*. 36:277–307.

Bordes, F., and D. Crabtree. 1969. The corbiac blade technique and other experiments. *Tebiwa*. 12(2):1–21.

Bowers, P. M. 1980. The Carlo Creek site: Geology and archaeology of an early Holocene site in the central Alaska Range. *Occasional Paper 27*. Fairbanks: Anthropology and Historic Preservation Cooperative Park Studies Unit, University of Alaska Fairbanks.

Butler, B. R. 1960. The old Cordilleran culture in the Pacific Northwest. *Idaho State University Museum Occasional Paper 5*.

Callahan, E. 1979. The basics of biface knapping in the eastern fluted point tradition: A manual for flintknappers and lithic analysts. *Archaeology of Eastern North America*. 7(1):1–180.

Clark, D. W. 1972. Archaeology of the Batza Tena obsidian source, west-central Alaska. *Anthropological Papers of the University of Alaska*. 15(2):1–21.

———. 1984a. Some practical applications of obsidian hydration dating in the subarctic. *Arctic*. 37(2):91–109.

———. 1984b. Northern fluted points: Paleo-eskimo, paleo-arctic, or paleo-Indian. *Canadian Journal of Anthropology*. 4(1):65–81.

Cole, D. 1985. *Captured Heritage: The Scramble for Northwest Coast Artifacts*. Seattle: University of Washington Press.

Cook, J. P. 1968. Some microblade cores from the western boreal forest. *Arctic Anthropology*. 5(1):121–127.

———. 1969. The early prehistory of Healy Lake, Alaska. Ph.D. Dissertation, University of Wisconsin. Ann Arbor: University Microfilms.

Cook, J. P., and T. E. Gillispie. 1986. Notched points and microblades. Manuscript in the possession of the author.

Cook, J. P., and R. A. McKennan. 1970. The village site at Healy Lake, Alaska: An interim report. Paper presented at the 35th Annual Meeting of the Society for American Archaeology, Mexico City.

Crabtree, D. E. 1967a. Notes on experiments in flintknapping: Tools used for making flaked stone artifacts. *Tebiwa*. 10:60–73.

———. 1967b. Notes on experiments in flintknapping: The flintknapper's raw materials. *Tebiwa*. 10:8–25.

Crabtree, D. E., and B. R. Butler. 1964. Notes on experiments in flintknapping: 1: Heat treatment of silica materials. *Tebiwa*. 7:1–42.

Del Bene, T. A. 1978. A microscopic analysis of wedge-shaped cores from the Alaskan sub-arctic: A preliminary study. Paper presented to the Tenth I.C.A.E.S. Prehistoric Technology Session.

———. 1980. Microscopic damage traces and manufacture process: The Denali complex example. *Lithic Technology*. 9:(2):34–35.

DeMent, J. A. 1962. The morphology and genesis of the subarctic brown forest soils of central Alaska. Ph.D. Dissertation, Cornell University.

Dikov, N. N. 1965. The stone age of Kamchatka and the Chukchi Peninsula in the light of new archaeological data. *Arctic Anthropology*. 3(1):10–25. (Translated by Gerald H. Clark from *Trudy Severo-Vostochnogo Kompleksnogo Navchno-Issledovatel'skogo Instituta*, 8:5–27, Magadan, 1964.)

Dixon, E. J. 1985. Cultural chronology of central interior Alaska. *Arctic Anthropology*. 22(1):47–66.

Dumond, D. E. 1977. *The Eskimos and Aleuts*. London: Thames and Hudson.

Epstein, J. F. 1963. The burin faceted projectile point. *American Antiquity*. 29(2):187–201.

Farthest North Collegian. 1934. Volume 12, number 12, pages 1, 8.

Flenniken, J. J. 1984. The past, present, and future of flintknapping: An anthropological perspective. *Annual Review of Anthropology*. 13:187–203.

Giddings, J. L., Jr. 1951. The Denbigh flint complex. *American Antiquity*. 16(3):193–202.

———. 1956. The burin spall artifact. *Arctic*. 9(4):229–237.

———. 1962. Alaska aboriginal culture: The national survey of historic sites and buildings theme XVI indigenous peoples and cultures special study. National Park Service.

Hartman, C. n.d. Fairbanks air temperature. Fairbanks: University of Alaska Institute of Water Resources.

Hayashi, K. 1968. The Fukui microblade technology and its relationships in northeast Asia and North America. *Arctic Anthropology*. 5(1):128–190.

Hayden, B., and J. Kamminga. 1979. An introduction to use-wear: The first CLUW. *Lithic Use-Wear Analysis*, edited by B. Hayden, 1–13. New York Academic Press.

Hester, T. R. 1972. Ethnographic evidence for the thermal alteration of siliceous stone. *Tebiwa*. 15(2): 63–65.

Holmes, C. E. 1978. Obsidian hydration studies: A preliminary report of results from central Alaska. Paper presented at the 31st Annual Northwest Anthropological Conference, Pullman.

———. 1986. Lake Minchumina prehistory: An archaeological analysis. *Aurora: Alaska Anthropological Association Monograph Series #2*.

Hosley, E. 1966. Interim report: Campus site archaeological investigations, 1966. Manuscript in the possession of the author.

———. 1968. The salvage excavation of the University of Alaska Campus site, 1967. Manuscript in the possession of the author.

Hosley, E., and J. Mauger. 1967. The Campus site excavations-1966. Paper presented at the Annual Meeting of the Society for American Archaeology, Ann Arbor.

Howard, E. B. 1935. Evidence of early man in North America. *Museum of the University of Pennsylvania*. 24(2–3).

Hrdlička, A. 1936. The coming of man from Asia in the light of recent discoveries. *Annual Report of the Smithsonian Institution, 1935*, 463–470.

Irving, W. N. 1953. Evidence of early tundra cultures in northern Alaska. *Anthropological Papers of the University of Alaska*. 1(2):55–85.

———. 1955. Burins from central Alaska. *American Antiquity*. 20(4):380–383.

Johnson, L. K., A. Richmond, and D. Combs. 1979. *Birch Hill Park: A Case Study of Interpretive Planning*. Fairbanks: University of Alaska Agricultural Experiment Station.

Kalin, J. 1981. Stem point manufacture and debitage recovery. *Archaeology of Eastern North America*. 9:134–175.

Keim, C. J. 1969. *Aghvook, White Eskimo: Otto Geist and Alaskan Archaeology*. College: University of Alaska Press.

Kobayashi, T. 1970. Microblade industries in the Japanese archipelago. *Arctic Anthropology*. 7(2):38–58.

Leechman, D. 1951. Bone grease. *American Antiquity*. 16(4):355–356.

Little, E. L., Jr., and L. A. Viereck. 1974. Guide to Alaska trees. *Agricultural Handbook 472*. Washington, D.C.: USDA Forest Service.

McCartney, A. P. 1977. Prehistoric human occupation of the Rat Islands. *The Environment of Amchitka Island, Alaska*, edited by M. L. Merritt and R. G. Fuller, Technical Information Center, Energy Research and Development Administration, TID-26712, 59–113.

MacNeish, R. S. 1959. A speculative framework of northern North American prehistory as of April 1959. *Anthropologica.* 1:1–17.

Maitland, R. E. 1986. The Chugwater site (FAI-035), Moose Creek Bluff, Alaska: Final Report, 1982 & 1983 Seasons. Report prepared for the U.S. Army Corps of Engineers, Alaska District, under contracts DACW85–84-M-0659 and DACW85–85-M-0494.

Mandeville, M. D., and J. J. Flenniken. 1974. A comparison of the flaking qualities of Nehawka chert before and after thermal treatment. *Plains Anthropologist.* 19:146–148.

Mauger, J. E. 1970. A study of Donnelly burins in the Campus archaeological collection. M.A. Thesis, Pullman: Washington State University.

———. 1971. The manufacture of Campus site microcores. Manuscript in the possession of the author.

Michels, J. W. 1984. Hydration rate constants for Batza Tena obsidian, Alaska. *Mohlab Technical Report 1,* State College, Pennsylvania.

———. 1985. Hydration rate constants for Alaska "group A" obsidian, Alaska. *Mohlab Technical Report 22,* State College, Pennsylvania.

Mobley, C. M. 1982. The Landmark Gap Trail site, Tangle Lakes, Alaska: Another perspective on the Amphitheater Mountain complex. *Arctic Anthropology.* 19(1):81–102.

———. 1983a. A statistical analysis of tipi ring diameters at sites near Santa Rosa, New Mexico. From Microcosm to Macrocosm: Advances in Tipi Ring Investigation and Interpretation, edited by L. B. Davis. *Memoirs of the Plains Anthropologist* 19: 101–112.

———. 1983b. A report to the Geist fund for the Campus site restudy project. Manuscript on file, University of Alaska Museum.

———. 1984. A report to the Alaska Historical Commission for the Campus site restudy project. Manuscript on file, Alaska Historical Commission, Anchorage.

———. 1985. A report to the Alaska Historical Commission for the Campus site restudy project. Manuscript on file, Alaska Historical Commission, Anchorage.

Mochanov, IU. A. 1969. The early neolithic of the Aldan. *Arctic Anthropology.* 6(1):95–103. (Translated by Roger Powers from *Sovetskaia Arkheologiia.* 2:126–136, Moscow, 1966).

Morlan, R. E. 1967. The pre-ceramic period of Hokkaido: An outline. *Arctic Anthropology.* 4(1): 164–220.

———. 1970. Wedge-shaped core technology in northern North America. *Arctic Anthropology.* 7(2):17–37.

———. 1973. A technological approach to lithic artifacts from Yukon Territory. *National Museum of Man Mercury Series Archaeological Survey of Canada Paper #7.* Ottawa.

———. 1978. Technological characteristics of some wedge-shaped cores in northwestern North America and northeast Asia. *Asian Perspectives.* 19(1): 96–106.

Morlan, V. 1971. The preceramic period of Japan: Honshu, Shikoku, and Kyushu. *Arctic Anthropology.* 8(1):136–170.

Nelson, N.C. 1926. The dune dwellers of the Gobi. *Natural History.* 26:246–251.

———. 1935. Early migration of man to America. *Natural History.* 35(4):356.

———. 1937. Notes on cultural relations between Asia and America. *American Antiquity.* 2:267–272.

Newcomer, M. H. 1971. Some quantitative experiments in handaxe manufacture. *World Archaeology.* 3(1):85–93.

Nie, N. H., C. H. Hull, J. G. Jenkins, K. Steinbrenner, and D. H. Bent. 1975. *Statistical Package for the Social Sciences: Second Edition.* New York: McGraw-Hill Book Company.

Orth, D. J. 1967. *Dictionary of Alaska Place Names.* Washington, D.C.: United States Government Printing Office.

Patton, W., Jr., and T. P. Miller. 1970. A possible bedrock source for obsidian found in archaeological sites in northwest Alaska. *Science.* 169:760–761.

Péwé, T. L. 1965a. Resume of the Quaternary geology of the middle Tanana River valley. *Guidebook for Field Conference F-Central and South Central Alaska,* 36–54, edited by T. L. Péwé, O. J. Ferrians, Jr., D. R. Nichols, and T. N. L. Karlstrom. International Association for Quaternary Research, 7th Congress, U.S.A. Lincoln: Nebraska Academy of Science.

———. 1965b. Resume of the Quaternary Geology of the Fairbanks Area. *Guidebook for Field Conference F-Central and South Central Alaska,* 6–36, edited by T. L. Péwé, O. J. Ferrians, Jr., D. R. Nichols, and T. N. L. Karlstrom. International Association for Quaternary Research, 7th Congress, U.S.A. Lincoln: Nebraska Academy of Science.

———. 1975a. Quaternary stratigraphic nomenclature in central Alaska. *United States Geological Survey Professional Paper 832.*

———. 1975b. Quaternary geology of Alaska. *United States Geological Survey Professional Paper 835.*

Péwé, T. L., J. W. Bell, R. B. Forbes, and F. R. Weber. 1975. *Geologic Map of the Fairbanks D-2 SE Quadrangle, Alaska.* Washington, D.C.: United States Geological Survey.

Pitzer, J. M. 1977. A guide to the identification of burins in prehistoric chipped stone assemblages. *University* of Texas at San Antonio Center for Archaeological Research Guidebook in Archaeology #1.

Powers, W. R., and J. F. Hoffecker. 1989. Late Pleistocene settlement in the Nenana valley, central Alaska. *American Antiquity*. 54(2):263–287.

Purdy, B. A., and K. K. Brooks. 1971. Thermal alteration of silica materials: An archaeological approach. *Science*. 173:322–325.

Rainey, F. 1939. Archaeology in central Alaska. *Anthropological Papers of the American Museum of Natural History*. 36(4):355–405.

———. 1940. Archaeological investigations in central Alaska. *American Antiquity*. 5(4):299–308.

———. 1953. The significance of recent archaeological discoveries in inland Alaska. *Memoirs of the Society for American Archaeology*. 9:43–46.

Rieger, S., J. A. DeMent, and D. Sanders. 1963. Soil survey of Fairbanks, Alaska. *USDA Soil Conservation Service Series 1959 25*.

Roberts, D. 1983. Bradford Washburn. *American Photographer*. April, 44–59.

Roosevelt, A., Jr., 1988. *For Lust of Knowing: The Memoirs of an Intelligence Officer in the Middle East*. Boston: Little Brown.

Sampson, C. G. (editor). 1978. *Paleoecology and Archaeology of an Acheulian Site at Caddington, England*. Dallas: Southern Methodist University Department of Anthropology.

Sanger, D. 1968a. The High River microblade industry, Alberta. *Plains Anthropologist*. 13(41):190–208.

———. 1968b. Prepared core and blade traditions in the Pacific Northwest. *Arctic Anthropology*. 5(1):92–120.

———. 1970. Mid-latitude core and blade traditions. *Arctic Anthropology*. 7(2):106–116.

Sanger, D., R. McGhee, and D. Wyatt. 1970. Appendix I: Blade description. *Arctic Anthropology*. 7(2):115–117.

Sheets, P. D., and G. R. Muto. 1972. Pressure blades and total cutting edge: An experiment in lithic technology. *Science*. 175:632–634.

Shinkwin, A. D. 1979. Daka De'nin's village and the Dixthada site: A contribution to northern Athapaskan prehistory. *National Museum of Man Mercury Series Archaeological Survey of Canada Paper 91*.

Smith, C. S. 1960. Manufacture of gunflints in France. *The Missouri Archaeologist*. 22:40–49.

Smith, J. W. 1974. The northeast Asian-northwest American microblade tradition (NANAMT). *Journal of Field Archaeology*. 1(3/4):347–364.

SPSS Inc. 1986. *SPSSX User's Guide: Edition 2*. Chicago: SPSS Inc.

Stahle, D. W., and J. E. Dunn. 1984. An analysis and application of the size distribution of waste flakes from the manufacture of bifacial stone tools. *World Archaeology*. 14(1):84–96.

Toth, N. 1985. Archaeological evidence for preferential righthandedness in the lower and middle Pleistocene, and its possible implications. *Journal of Human Evolution*. 14:607–614.

Wahrhaftig. C. 1965. Physiographic divisions of Alaska. *United States Geological Survey Professional Paper 482*.

West, F. H. 1967. The Donnelly Ridge site and the definition of an early core and blade complex in central Alaska. *American Antiquity*. 32(3):360–382.

———. 1975. Dating the Denali complex. *Arctic Anthropology*. 12:76–81.

———. 1980. *The Archaeology of Beringia*. New York: Columbia University Press.

Wheeler, M. E., and D. W. Clark. 1977. Elemental characterization of obsidian from the Koyukuk River, Alaska, by atomic absorption spectrophotometry. *Archaeometry*. 19(1):15–31.

Witthoft, J. 1966. A history of gunflints. *Pennsylvania Archaeologist*. 36(1–2):12–49.

Wood, W. R., and D. L. Johnson. 1978. A survey of disturbance processes in archaeological site formation. *Advances in Archaeological Method and Theory, Volume I*, edited by M. B. Schiffer, 315–381. New York: Academic Press.

Woodward, A. 1960. Some notes on gunflints. *Missouri Archaeologist*. 22:29–39.

Workman, W. B. 1974. First dated traces of early Holocene man in the southwest Yukon Territory, Canada. *Arctic Anthropology*. 11 (Supplement):94–103.

———. 1978. Prehistory of the Aishihik-Kluane area, southwest Yukon Territory. *National Museum of Man Mercury Series Archaeological Survey of Canada Paper 74*.

Wyatt, D. 1970. Microblade attribute patterning: A statistical examination. *Arctic Anthropology*. 7(2):97–105.